Lincoln

– Townscapes through Time –

Text by Michael J. Jones

Paintings by Peter Rooke

Cottage
Publications

First published by Cottage Publications,
an imprint of Laurel Cottage Ltd.
Donaghadee, N. Ireland 2010.
Copyrights Reserved.
© Illustrations by Peter Rooke 2010.
© Text by Michael Jones 2010.
All rights reserved.
No part of this book may be reproduced or stored on any media
without the express written permission of the publishers.
Design & origination in Northern Ireland.
Printed & bound in China.
ISBN 978 1 900935 84 5

The Author

A native of South Yorkshire, Mick Jones studied Classics then undertook research in Roman Archaeology at the University of Manchester. He has since spent almost all his professional life in Lincoln; for over twenty years directing the city's Archaeology Unit before becoming City Archaeologist in 2000. His primary research interests are in the Roman and Early Medieval periods, and he has written several books and excavation reports on aspects of Lincoln, as well as many articles.

He holds honorary positions at Bishop Grosseteste University College in Lincoln and the University of Nottingham, and has taught undergraduate courses at both institutions. He is keen to promote the interest and value of Lincoln's heritage to the local community and visitors alike. He is an active member and the current President of the Society for Lincolnshire History and Archaeology, and also chairs the Survey of Lincoln Project.

One day soon he hopes to retire and see more of his family and grandchildren.

The Artist

Peter Rooke studied art full time covering various aspects at a foundation course before deciding to concentrate on Technical Illustration. He went on to work in a commercial environment including in the motor industry, contract studios and as a government employee before taking retirement.

From 1995 Peter has been concentrating on paintings in watercolour and pastels, preferring the immediacy and spontaneity of these mediums. His work is mainly landscapes and townscapes with influences coming from the many walks he enjoys around the country, as well from as artists such as Turner and Crawhall. Peter has had several successful exhibitions with many paintings in private collections around the world. He has also exhibited at the Mall Galleries and appeared on Channel 4's *Watercolour Challenge*.

Peter is now part of a co-operative that is Harding House Gallery in Lincoln, and takes an active part in running the gallery as well as having his work on permanent display.

Contents

Lincoln: an Introduction

Lincolnshire – the historic county that extends from the southern bank of the Humber estuary almost to Peterborough – is a huge tract of land, as long north-south as is the distance from its southern tip to London. In travelling eastwards from its western boundary all the way to the coast, one encounters several different landscapes: from the Trent valley to the 'Lincoln Edge', the steep western scarp of the Jurassic limestone ridge, then a wide but shallow clay vale before the rolling chalk Wolds, and finally the coastal marsh. To characterise the county's landscape as a monotonous plain, as many do, is therefore misleading. It is an impression based largely on the nature of the land reclaimed from the sea: the coastal zone and to a greater extent the fenland of its south-eastern quarter. The fens are as much a feature of Cambridgeshire and Norfolk as of Lincolnshire.

This spacious county of 'big skies' is, for the most part, sparsely populated, with the only sizeable conurbations being at Scunthorpe and Grimsby in the north and at Lincoln itself. Apart from these three, which grew particularly during the

19th century as a result of industrial development, the most significant centres are those at Boston, Spalding, Grantham, Gainsborough, Sleaford, Louth and Horncastle. Skegness is the largest of the popular coastal resorts. There are countless villages, large and small, and many of them attractive in terms of their setting and architecture. For all its size and charms, Lincolnshire is a generally under-visited and under-appreciated county, much now given over to producing the nation's food, including the vast acres of vegetables that led to the poet John Betjeman's description as *'the smell of rotting cabbages'*.

Lincoln is a common place-name of which most people have heard, but that familiarity stems partly from the famous American president, after whom many towns in North America were named, and subsequently brands of motor-cars, biscuits and other products. An eponymous college of Oxford University was founded by a bishop of Lincoln. The legendary outlaw Robin Hood and his associates wore 'Lincoln green'. The original Lincoln was a regional centre for a combined period of perhaps seven centuries in all, and at times played a significant role in national events. It was the home, or at least local town, for some important figures, from the vastly wealthy Aaron the Jew, the wealthiest person in late 12th century England, to the mathematician George Boole, who was born and worked in the city before his academic career as a pioneer in algebra that led to the development of the computer. Others, including Cardinal Wolsey, Henry VIII's Chancellor,

had spent part of their earlier careers here, while the botanist Sir Joseph Banks, whose family inherited a large estate in the county, was a regular visitor even though his duties as long-time President of the Royal Society demanded his presence in the capital.

Its apogee as a regional capital was reached in the Roman period (mid-1st to 4th centuries AD), and again in the Anglo-Scandinavian and High Medieval periods (c. 900-1300). Since about 1300, the city has been part of a region governed from elsewhere, as it had been for much of the Anglo-Saxon period as part of Northumbria and then Mercia. It again boomed in the 19th century as a fast-growing centre of heavy industry, but never expanded to the size of the principal metropoleis such as Birmingham and Manchester. Present-day Lincoln is a relatively small city in terms of its population size, and attracts fewer visitors than some comparable places, owing mainly to its location away from the main routes northwards. The Roman roads that once converged on Lincoln may still be a feature of the modern network, but since a 12th century bishop of Lincoln constructed a bridge over the Trent at Newark, it has lain about 15 miles to the east of the main road northwards, now the A1. At the time of writing, it has very limited direct rail services to London – although this temporary aberration is due to be corrected with their partial reinstatement from 2011.

Yet it is one of the most distinctive cities in Europe. That special quality applies both to its approach, enhanced by the way that the Cathedral towers over the town, and to the actual experience of the historic centre, a felicitous combination of natural topography and remarkable architectural survivals from the past two thousand years. This environment is enjoyed by the local community and visitors alike, never more intensively than at the Christmas Market in early December, attended by up to 200,000 people over four days. Yet, for much of the time, the historic centre can be relatively peaceful, and that is part of its charm. The various paintings by Peter Rooke in this volume provide an excellent impression of the historic and architectural richness of Lincoln as a place, but represent only a part of the urban life: the city offers many other sites and sights to discover and enjoy.

Visitors, Commentators and Scholars

Lincoln has attracted visitors since it first existed, and in many cases they stayed here for a long period. Those who did include the thousands of Roman legionaries from much nearer to the Mediterranean, and the traders who followed them and also formed an important element of the later Roman civic population. The inscribed stone found at Mainz in Germany that dates the foundation of Lincoln as a colony was set up by a man who was both a citizen of Lincoln and who had also served as the chief centurion of a legion – but not one of those based at Lincoln. Other inscriptions from the city document various traders, some of them with international links back to Gaul and Greece. A military-bureaucratic elite arrived with the choice of the city to be the capital of new province covering the East Midlands and part of East Anglia in the 4th century. Subsequent centuries saw invaders from Germany, Denmark and Normandy. Our only documented accounts belong to a later period, when travelling scholars began to record their impressions. These accounts begin in the late 16th century with the antiquary John Leland, and were initially confined to the historic remains.

The vicissitudes of Lincoln's history had bequeathed monuments in stone to not so prosperous eras: strong Roman walls and gates, and the great medieval monuments, as well as remains of houses, churches and religious houses. By the late 17th and early 18th centuries when, along with landscape artists, these visitors became more frequent, much of the city was being rebuilt and expanded, but other areas were in a sorry state. One memorable account noted that fragments of ruined medieval structures were even being used for pig-sties. That decay was remarked on by John Evelyn in 1654 and by Abraham de la Pryme in 1690. The later comments by Daniel Defoe echoed their words, and are the most frequently quoted; while he found the area above the hill congenial, the lower part of the city was *ancient, ragged, decayed, and still decaying*. Much was soon to be swept away by the industrialisation and rapid expansion of the next two hundred years.

The study of Lincoln's past may have had a long history in itself, but was only put on a firm footing from the middle of the 20th century, with the publication of *Medieval Lincoln* (1948), the first of Sir Francis Hill's four substantial books, and the establishment of an organisation to investigate the city's archaeological remains on a systematic basis. Much has been achieved since, in terms of both historical research and archaeological discoveries, and more recently with their public interpretation, something that should only be undertaken after the serious research has been carried out. As well as Hill's books, there have been important scholarly studies of documents, buildings and place-names. Lincoln has benefited not only from some distinguished professional historians, but also the work of a number of local enthusiasts researching into various aspects.

For much of Lincoln's long past, however, archaeology is our principal source. A professional 'digging' team was established in 1972. Over the next quarter-century it undertook more excavations and produced more data than all previous work in the city. There are rich pickings in the city, with deposits in places 5 metres or more deep, reflecting the fact that at least half a million people in all have lived in the area of the present city over the past few thousand years and inadvertently left us the benefit of their debris. The analysis of this material has enabled us to obtain a more balanced picture of the past than was possible from the study of purely documen-

tary sources, or from examining the major monuments. It allows us to recognise the lifestyles of the poorer classes and to understand the contemporary environment, as well as to fill in several chronological gaps. For instance, we now have evidence of occupation dating to before the Roman conquest, and we understand better the nature of the place between the Roman and Norman periods. Moreover, archaeological methods are being applied to the physical remains of the modern period. Even now, at a time when there is pressure to preserve below-ground evidence *in situ* rather than investigate large areas, significant discoveries are still being made.

THE CITY IN PROSPECT

Lincoln may never again be in the first rank of British cities in terms of its size, or its football team achieve Premiership status. It is, nevertheless, a city; a complex settlement with many facets to life – artistic culture and religion as well as shopping and sport. Moreover, it regularly scores highly in United Kingdom polls both as a place to live and one to visit. Its greatest distinction is its historic fabric, notably the Castle and Cathedral that are so prominent on the hilltop, and that part of the city in their shadow. But there are also many gems in other parts of town, some of them practically hidden away and not well known even to local people. The preservation, study and interpretation of this outstanding heritage have, in recent years, attracted huge amounts of investment, much of it in the form of grants from national organisations that recognise its value in educational, social and economic terms. The challenge for future generations will be to maintain, interpret and enhance Lincoln's special historic character so that it can be enjoyed by generations to come. I hope that this book, in its small way, contributes to that goal.

The Cathedral Chapter House, built from the 1220s, is a striking building, its weight carried on a central pillar supporting twenty stone ribs, with eight flying buttresses acting as a counterweight. It is ten-sided, with the double entrance on the west (from the cloister). The stained-glass windows depict the Cathedral's story from the time of its construction until John Wesley's visit in 1790. Its primary function was for formal gatherings of the Dean and Chapter, and here also the English Parliament met on several occasions – in 1301, 1316 and 1327, as King Edward I was occupied with wars with the Scots. In recent years it has been used along with the nave as a film-set, and housed a display for a while about the film *The Da Vinci Code,* in which Lincoln stood in for Westminster Abbey.

The Chapter House lies over the site of the Roman city ditch; to the south, the bishop had to obtain permission from the King to demolish the city wall in 1255 in order to build the Angel Choir. The wall itself ran to the right of this view, beneath the front of what is now the Cathedral's coffee shop, beneath the Library, while the Close Wall formerly ran across the line in front of the Chapter House. This view is taken from Eastgate, and remains of one of the Roman gate-towers can be seen across the street. The medieval gateway that replaced it served as apartments for Bishop Alexander prior to the construction of the Episcopal palace in the mid-12th century.

In the foreground, where houses once stood, is G. F. Watts' 1905 marble statue of the Poet Laureate, Alfred Lord Tennyson (1809-92), along with his dog, a Siberian wolfhound. Tennyson was brought up at Somersby in the Lincolnshire Wolds and was inspired by the countryside around his home.

The Chapter House and Tennyson's statue

LINCOLN

P. Rooke 10

As the Dean and Chapter continued the process of buying up property adjacent to the Cathedral for its various officers, the sites of the three houses visible here (numbers 10, 11 and 12 Minster Yard) passed into its ownership in the late 13th century. All retain fabric from that period, but were subsequently rebuilt.

As its neighbours to the north, No. 10 (the former Choristers' House) belongs to the post-medieval period. An account of 1649 refers to a building with an impressive 8-yard span. The choristers were housed in accommodation to the rear. The present front range is of 1661-2, in the vernacular tradition of that period found along the limestone band that extends to the Cotswolds.

Next door (No. 11) became the Chancery, the residence of the Cathedral Chancellor, from the time of Antony Bek in 1321. Katherine Swynford, the mistress of John of Gaunt, the Earl of Lancaster (from whom the Tudor dynasty was later descended) lived here in the 1380s after they had separated. John subsequently obtained a Papal Dispensation allowing them to marry. On his death soon afterwards, Katherine moved to the Priory (No. 2 Minster Yard). The 13th century north gable of the Chancery survives to provide some clue to the quality of the house, and there are 14th century elements to the rear. The present

frontage, the earliest brick building in the city, dates from the end of the 15th century. It has a large chamber with an impressive oriel window, over a semi-basement.

To its south is No. 12, known as Graveley Place. Though occupying only part of its former site, it was much rebuilt at the end of the 19th century, but incorporates some earlier elements. These include a blocked medieval doorway and corbels. To the right of this view, Minster Yard turns west and the street here becomes Pottergate, leading down to the gate in the Close.

The original Lincoln Imp can be found within the Cathedral, towards the eastern end of the Angel Choir. A legend suggests that he was turned to stone by the angels. Profits from copies of the imp made as souvenirs by the jeweller James Usher funded the building of the city's art gallery. Today, Lincoln's football club is known as the Red Imps.

THE FAMOUS
LINCOLN IMP

Minster Yard East
and the Chancery

LINCOLN

P. Rooke 10

The gardens in the foreground of this picture lie to the rear of the Usher Gallery. The gallery itself was built in 1926, but what became its grounds, named Temple Gardens after the imitation Greek temple visible on the right-hand side of the image, were first established over a century earlier. They had originally contained several trees. A grant from the Heritage Lottery Fund enabled the gardens (along with the Arboretum) to be given a makeover in 2003.

Beyond the grounds, and marked by the line of a high stone wall – the Close Wall – and ruinous structures further left, are the remains of the medieval Bishops' Palace. This was the site of the Bishop of Lincoln's residence from the time of its construction in the mid-12th century. The king made a grant of land in the north-eastern corner of the lower walled city, a little to the south of the Cathedral. The bishop could then enter the Cathedral through the south transept, and the circular window here is known as the 'Bishop's Eye'.

At this period, the bishop was extremely wealthy, with a large household, and two halls were provided, built either side of AD 1200, one for private purposes (to the east) and one for public events and banquets. There were also kitchens and storage areas. As greater comforts became available, the bishop installed them. A chapel range and adjacent tower were added in the 1430s by Robert Alnwick, and the tower, much restored in the late 19th century, is the highest surviving element of the Palace. Although the bishop could accommodate King Henry VIII in 1541, it was too badly damaged by a Civil War battle here in 1648 to serve its purpose and, within a century, stone was being removed for Cathedral repairs. Other palaces outside the city took over as the bishop's principal residence. The site is now in the care of English Heritage, which has in recent years improved the site's public presentation and added a modern garden on the southern terrace, adjacent to the city's vineyard.

The more intact stone buildings beyond the ruins on the left belong to Edward King House, named after the highly-regarded bishop who had this house erected as his residence in 1888. It now provides office and other accommodation for the diocese. The present bishop lives in Eastgate.

Medieval Bishops' Palace

FROM THE USHER GALLERY GROUNDS

P. Rooke 10

These attractive brick houses facing the west front of the Cathedral were erected towards the middle of the 18th century, and extend back almost to the line of the Close Wall, which formerly ran to the rear of what is now the White Hart Hotel. They gained their name from being the first in the city to be numbered. They all appear to be contemporary, but display slight variations, some as a result of later alterations. From their front windows they have a stupendous view of the towering frontage of the Cathedral.

To the south of Exchequergate lie the two houses often referred to as the former Sub-Deanery (No. 18 Minster Yard) and Deanery (No. 17); both have been occupied at various times by different members of the Cathedral Chapter. The former dates to c. 1870, the Deanery two centuries earlier, probably a partial rebuild on a similar plan of a 15th century house destroyed in the Civil War battle that took place hereabouts. Beneath number 18, adjacent to the gate, the remains of a Roman house with an underfloor heating system (hypocaust) were discovered while constructing a cellar in 1739. The then Clerk of Works, Thomas Sympson, a keen historian himself, called in a local antiquarian, Browne Willis. His notes were the basis of a pioneering survey produced by the Society of Antiquaries' official engraver, George Vertue, one of the first pictures to render accurately the stratigraphical perspective. The remains of the hypocaust can now only be accessed with difficulty.

To the east of number 17 (now the Cathedral Centre) is an area of raised garden overlying the line of the Close Wall, giving an excellent view towards both the south-western corner of the Cathedral and the medieval Bishops' Palace to the south.

The 'Number Houses'

AND THE WEST SIDE OF THE MINSTER YARD

P. Rooke 10

In 1285 the Bishop sought and received permission from the King to enclose by a wall the properties belonging to the Dean and Chapter. The resulting structure – the Close Wall – was commenced almost immediately but not completed for several decades. The best sections of that wall to survive can be found on the south side of the Cathedral, to the north of the medieval Bishops' Palace, and along Winnowsty Lane, linking two impressive towers. Another long stretch lies along East Bight, enclosing the Bishop's garden, but has been much re-built. The Close Wall was provided with a number of gateways, few of which now survive. There are indications of two of them to the east of the Cathedral: Pottergate retains much of its appearance, although having been restored in 1884, and the wall either side was breached to open it to modern-day traffic. Priorygate, further north, is an 1816 rebuild to a much narrower scale, a shadow of its medieval predecessor. Three other gates stood on Eastgate, one adjacent to the site of the former Roman gate, while a postern is still to be found on Greestone Stairs.

The most impressive of them all is Exchequergate, which lies in front of the west front of the Cathedral. Even this is only one element of what had been a double gate: several depictions survive of the western Exchequergate before the outer gate's demolition from 1796. The double gates were completed around 1320, and the surviving gate was cleaned as a gesture to European Architectural Heritage Year in 1975. This too had three storeys and three archways, with both diagonal and ridge ribs visible in their vaulting. The structure also incorporates some of the earliest brick to be used in the medieval city. There were once shops here, and the rooms above are currently used in part as a centre for historical research.

Exchequergate and the Close

LINCOLN

P. Rooke '10

The square, whose official address is Castle Hill, set between the main entrance to Lincoln Castle and Exchequergate with the Cathedral behind, is surely one of the most delightful urban spaces in Europe. It forms an ideal focus for Lincoln's celebrated Christmas Market, a regular fixture here for the past thirty years and, though much imitated, still one of the most popular in Britain. Up to 200,000 people are estimated to visit during its four-day opening in early December each year; local hotels are fully booked by the previous January. The square had accommodated a vegetable market in the 19th century and, during the rest of the year, still has regular specialist stalls.

There are buildings of several eras here, apart from the medieval Exhequergate. On the north side of the gate is St. Mary Magdalene church, fronting on the southern end of Bailgate. It was originally built in the last decades of the 13th century, but what survives belongs either to a 1695 rebuild or largely to that of 1882, to the design of the Victorian architect G. F. Bodley. The interior only has a narrow north aisle. This church is often open at least for viewing.

On the south side of the gate are a number of shops and, on the corner with Steep Hill, the pub known as the Magna Carta, formerly a restaurant of the same name. The reference is appropriate, as the Cathedral owns, and the Castle displays, the Lincoln exemplar of the famous medieval document to which King John was compelled to agree. This is one – and probably the best preserved – of only four original documents to survive from 1215, as among the witnesses was the Bishop of Lincoln. It is hugely admired, especially in North America and in Australia, as the founding document for a number of western democracies.

Across from St. Mary Magdalene at the south end of Bailgate is the half-timbered Leigh-Pemberton House, built in the 16th century and currently in use in part as a Tourist Information Centre. To its west is an attractive early 18th century house used as offices, and then the lighter brick of the Judges' Lodgings, built in 1810. This building long served as accommodation for the Crown Court judges presiding in the Castle, but that is no longer the case, and occasional cultural and social events now take place here.

Castle Hill

LINCOLN

P. Rooke '10

Bailgate is one of the city's most attractive and endearing streets, its charm based on the small scale and variety of its buildings. In the southern part of the street shown here, looking southwards towards Castle Hill, its route is sinuous, varying considerably from that of its Roman predecessor – the *cardo,* or principal street, also the line of the Roman road from London to York. As a result, excavations have encountered remains of Roman buildings, including the frontage of the civic centre (forum) in the form of a row of columns. They were first discovered during work on new cellars at Nos. 28-29, but most were revealed when sewers were being installed in the 1890s. Their locations are marked in the modern street surface. In contrast, the cellar of No. 8, part of the former Antelope Inn, displays evidence in its basement of the blocked Roman sewer that had run beneath the centre of the Roman street. A stretch of the former sewer was opened specially in 1848 for the annual meeting of the Archaeological Institute, a major social event that lasted a week, but access since has been difficult to arrange.

The name of the street is derived from the fact that it lay within the outer bailey of the Castle. The buildings shown here represent the combination of shops, pubs and restaurants that characterise the area. Most of the visible fabric is of the 18th- or early 19th century, but these structures are derived from medieval predecessors, and some still contain remains of several different centuries. In the distance can be seen the White Hart Hotel and beyond that St. Mary Magdalene church at the corner of Castle Hill. At the time of writing, the whole street is being given a makeover, with a new pedestrian-friendly surface.

The Newport Arch lies at the northern end of Bailgate; it was the inner arch of the Roman north gate.

NEWPORT ARCH

Bailgate

LINCOLN

CORDON ROAD

P. Rooke 10

The striking porticoed south range of the former Lawn hospital was largely hidden for more than a century, and even now that it is a public area it is too little visited. Its site lies immediately outside the west gate of the Castle, and in the Roman and medieval periods was occupied at times, but was never a significant suburb. Excavations have, however, revealed Roman traders' houses and burials, and we know that in the medieval period this area took the literal name of 'Westcastle', served by St. Bartholomew's church and the nearby St. Leonard's hospital. Here too was the 'Battle Place', where legal disputes were settled and punishment, including by hanging, were meted out until c. 1815.

Soon after this date, in 1819-20, the Lawn asylum was opened, with funding raised partly by Dr Francis Willis (who had treated King George III). The prime mover was Dr Edward Parker Charlesworth; his statue stands in the grounds at the corner of Union Road and Carline Road. Over more than three decades, Dr Charlesworth pioneered methods of treatment involving less physical restraint and abolished solitary confinement. These advances attracted many specialist observers, and had wide influence.

The original building, designed by Richard Ingleman, was later extended. There were over 100 inmates and 25 staff in 1841, but many of the pauper patients were transferred to a new facility that opened in Bracebridge Heath in 1852. This allowed more space and scope for recreational activity. Funds were often scarce, but further extensions were added for catering purposes in 1893, while a separate nurses' home was built in 1938. The hospital was eventually closed by the NHS in 1985 as national policy shifted to 'Care in the Community'.

The whole complex was purchased by the City Council, and formally opened in November 1990 by HRH the Prince of Wales as a conference and cultural centre. The opening event was a conference on Archaeology in Historic Towns, at which the Government launched its new policy for archaeology. It still functions as the venue for meetings and weddings, and contains a few shops as well as the Sir Joseph Banks Conservatory, named after the distinguished Lincolnshire-based botanist. The nurses' home became a centre for the City's archaeology team, including an educational display, but is now a hotel.

The Lawn

LINCOLN

P. Rooke '10

The Castle that now occupies the south-western quarter of the upper Roman city might not have been built in that form before the early 12th century: it has been suggested that William the Conqueror's first castle at Lincoln, from 1068, consisted of the whole of the upper Roman enclosure, provided with new gates, perhaps the present motte in the south-western corner, and a tower which also formed a new west front for the Cathedral. During its active use, the Castle was prominent in several battles in the city, including the dispute between Stephen and Matilda in the 1140s, and the 'Battle of Lincoln Fair' in 1217 when the barons sided with the French. Even though it was in need of repair by 1327, it was a key target again during the Civil War (1642-8).

The building shown here faces visitors to the Castle on entering through the main (east) gate. It is the Crown Court, built in 1823-6 in a 'Gothick' style with turrets, replacing an earlier Shire Hall that had stood for only about 50 years. The county gaol building on the south side of the route to the courts was at first T-shaped when built in 1787 to replace a predecessor reported as being in very poor condition. It was arranged along lines recommended by the prison reformer John Howard. An extension to the rear was built in 1847-8; this brought better facilities for the prisoners, but introduced at the same time was the 'separate system' that minimised human contact. This principle can be best appreciated by visiting the chilling prison chapel. The gaol has survived more or less in the form that it took when was replaced by a new prison on Greetwell Road in 1878. It also contains a display centering on the Lincoln exemplar of the Magna Carta, a significant document for western democracies that attracts visitors from far and wide.

A tour of the walls, some at elevated level, allows views around and beyond the city as well as visits to the two keeps, the two gates and Cobb Hall at the north-eastern corner. This tower's basement served as a dungeon before the prison was erected. Its roof was used for thirty-eight hangings between about 1815 and the 1860s, often with crowds numbering thousands to watch the spectacle. Also within the grounds are the bath-house that served the prison and the remains of a statue of George III. The 'Lucy Tower' keep was used for prisoners' burials from 1829, and some headstones survive. The Observatory Tower in the south-eastern keep was erected around 1815-20 by the prison governor John Merryweather to support his enthusiasm for astronomy.

The Castle

LINCOLN

P. Rooke 10

Steep Hill is another delightful street in architectural terms. For those minded, it also offers good-quality merchandise as well as pubs, cafés and restaurants, some of them established and popular fixtures in the life of the city. This view shows principally the range of buildings down the west side as far as Wordsworth Street and, as well as being pleasing to the eye, they provide much of historical and architectural interest. Aaron the Jew's house might have been hereabouts in the late 12th century: the south-eastern keep of the Castle, to the rear of these properties, was referred to as 'Aaron's tower'. Some still contain medieval fabric, in particular the row of former shops consisting of Nos. 26-29: the rear range of the recently-restored pub now named Widow Cullen's Well consists of the former medieval hall. Others date principally to the 18th or 19th century. There were at times other ale-houses in this group, including Nos. 32 and 33. A plaque on the wall of No. 33 records the fact that it was a common haunt of T. E. Lawrence, author of *Seven Pillars of Wisdom,* when visiting Lincoln.

At No. 26 is a fragment of stone wall that actually represents a curtailed element of the wall and south gate of the upper Roman city, more of which can be found opposite (within No. 44 Steep Hill). There was a medieval gate, long demolished, a little to the south of the Roman structure. Wordsworth Street is a relatively late intrusion into the streetscape, inserted in the 1880s.

Steep Hill upper (west side)

LINCOLN

P. Rooke 10

Below the Magna Carta public house the range of buildings here is again of considerable historic interest as well as variety. Among them is the half-timbered popular café, formerly a pair of tenements built under one roof c. 1600. All of them lie over the eastern part of the main street of the Roman city (Ermine Street), having encroached westwards from the line of the medieval Close Wall. At the bottom of this range is No. 44, formerly the Leopard Inn.

18th century depictions of this particular location indicate that the springing of a Roman gate-arch was still in place, but understanding the plan of the gate has proved more problematic. A major step forward came in 2001 when work on no. 44 revealed both part of the east side of what must have been the eastern carriageway – confirming that it was a double gate – and the spina, which carried the two arches. These are both partially visible within the shop, which also has a deep cellar cut into the bedrock. Unlike other locations in the city, the Roman levels have not become deeply buried here: the need to take wheeled vehicles beneath the surviving arch meant that the original ground-level had to be more or less maintained.

Outside No. 45 is the parish boundary marker between St. Michael-on-the-Mount and St. Mary Magdalene, as well as the entrance to the Bail: the outer bailey of the Castle, lying within the upper city walls, was subject to the control of the county constable on behalf of the Crown.

Steep Hill upper (east side)

LINCOLN

A little below the site of the gates on Steep Hill is one of Lincoln's most historic structures. This is the Norman House, a double-ranged building (the south gable of the rear range can be seen from Christ's Hospital Terrace) of the later 12th century. It displays some original features both internally and externally, although the twin window was re-set in 1878. This house may have been the residence of the Jew Joceus of York. It was formerly, but erroneously, associated with Aaron the Jew, perhaps the most famous moneylender of his day, whose house was actually a little further up the hill. When he died in 1186, a special branch of the Exchequer had to be opened to deal with the money owing to him, some from the highest levels of society. A recent survey judged him to have been in the top ten of Britain's wealthiest ever citizens!

The open space to the south may have originated as one of the city's markets created around the time of the Norman conquest; the fish market lay here or a little to the west, while the cloth and skin markets lay further down Michaelgate. It is also here that the two medieval streets of Michaelgate (the medieval Parchemingate) and Steep Hill (the medieval Mikelgate) met back on the Roman line after deviating in order to ease the gradient. The Roman route, for pedestrians at least, had gone straight up the hill, with flights of steps, while wheeled traffic had to take a zig-zag course.

On higher ground to the west, along the south side of Wordsworth Street – a late 19th century insertion into the streetscape – is Chad Varah House, built in 1777 as the County Hospital then used for many decades as the Lincoln Theological College. It is currently part of the University of Lincoln. Chad Varah had trained here for the Church of England, and on the basis of his experience in the city had subsequently established the Samaritans organisation.

Among the buildings along Christ's Hospital Terrace itself is the former Bluecoat School of 1784, a building also currently used for educational purposes. To its south is the site and former churchyard of the medieval parish church of St. Michael. Its Victorian successor of 1855-6 still stands, though no longer used as a church. More prominent in this picture is the distinctive Harlequin, a former inn dating back to the late 15th century with many later elements. To the right on Michaelgate is another half-timbered structure, 42 Michaelgate, which can be rented as a holiday let.

The Norman House and the Harlequin

LINCOLN

P. Rooke 10

This view is a useful corrective to those who believe that Lincolnshire is an entirely flat county. The situation of the city of Lincoln, at a glacial gap in the Jurassic limestone ridge, means that there are steep scarps to the south (at South Common), and to the north, as here, as well as for many miles along the Lincoln Edge to the west. The ground-level rises from the river, at about 5 metres above sea level, to the giddy height of about 65 metres at the junction of Bailgate with Westgate. A walk up High Street, The Strait and Steep Hill itself is the way to experience this gradient most directly. Even then, the present route is a medieval deviation from the main Roman highway for pedestrians, which ascended the hill directly in occasional flights of monumental steps. Remains of them were found in the gardens to the rear of the buildings on the left.

The view here is taken from below the point where the street of Danesgate, probably an early medieval short-cut from the lower east gate (the 'Clasketgate'), joins on to Steep Hill. It might have originated as one element of the Roman vehicular route that zig-zagged its way up the steeper part of the hill. This location was known as the 'Mayor's Chair', from the construction of the embankment in 1732 to allow porters a rest and enable vehicles running out of control a gentler route via Danesgate.

Along this part of Steep Hill was the medieval poultry market, one of several different specialist markets lining the streets outside the upper south gate. As with much of Steep Hill and Bailgate, the buildings along the street are mainly of the 18th and 19th century, some of them incorporating earlier elements. The large stone building with a half-timbered first floor is Harding House, itself much rebuilt and restored. It is the subject of a bequest that stipulates that it can only be used for arts and crafts purposes. It currently showcases the work of a number of local artists, including that of Peter Rooke, who has produced the watercolours that illustrate the present volume. Mr Harding himself was a collector of many of the antiquities found during building works in the city centre.

Steep Hill (lower) including Harding House

LINCOLN

P. Rooke 10

Adjacent to what was the medieval corn market, and opposite what was the parish church of St. Cuthbert, these two important survivals stand adjacent at the foot of Steep Hill. They are often considered together, but are in fact considerably different in age. To the left, the Jew's House is documented as the house of a Jewish merchant: the Jewish community served as the bankers of the medieval city. It has two storeys, with a hall on the upper floor, and was probably built in the period 1150-70, when stone began to be used again for domestic residences, as well as for churches. Its completeness makes it a building of national significance. Especially remarkable is the sculpture of the string-course and the interlaced chain-link pattern around the doorway. It may originally have had an arcaded frontage for shops. Three original doorways survive within. There were shops here for centuries, until recent decades, but in recent years, it has been used mainly as a restaurant.

By contrast, Jews' Court to its north, although also of stone, is principally of the 17th-18th centuries, though probably replacing a house roughly contemporary with its neighbour. A tradi-

tion has associated it with a Jewish synagogue known from documents to have stood next to the Jew's House and where a Jewish wedding took place in 1296. It is, however, more likely on grounds of analogy with examples elsewhere that the synagogue lay discreetly to the rear of the street frontage, in a 'court'

behind the Jew's House. Just such an arrangement existed near to the top of High Street, on its west side, where a synagogue is documented on Hungate to its rear.

This was a poor area of the city a century or so ago. Jews' Court was occupied by several tenements containing about 20 people in all, and was listed as due for slum clearance in 1928. It was saved by an offer from the Lincolnshire Architectural and Archaeological Society, which restored it in 1931-2. It is now used successfully as the headquarters of that society's successor, the Society for Lincolnshire History and Archaeology, and contains a bookshop covering all aspects of the county's past.

The Jew's House and Jews' Court

LINCOLN

P. Rooke 10

At the top of the High Street, the modern routes diverge from the Roman line, either towards St. Martin's Square to the west, or through the narrows of the appropriately named The Strait. As with a similarly narrow medieval street in York, here was the meat 'shambles'. The medieval plots largely remain, as well as some of the fabric, but much was subsequently rebuilt, and for centuries has contained a variety of shops. In the 19th and early 20th centuries, people were also crowded into courts and yards to the rear of these frontages.

Excavations took place in the 1970s at the junction with Danes Terrace, now the housing scheme known as Neustadt Court, named after Lincoln's twin city in Germany. They revealed that there had been solid stone houses along the street front in the 13th century, but that these had been largely replaced in the 16th and 17th centuries, some incorporating reused medieval stonework from demolished houses or churches. Just below the point from which this view was produced, a jettied late 15th century building, Dernstall House, can be seen. It was much rebuilt in 1970, one of several such projects undertaken by the Lincoln Civic Trust.

This stretch of street might fairly be described as the entrance to the historic core favoured by visitors, with its small-scale shops and regular opportunities for refreshment. The houses visible towards the end of this view sit over the site of the former St. Cuthbert's church, in the medieval cornmarket, and opposite the Jew's House and Jews' Court. The house named St.

Cuthbert's Lodge perpetuates the parish name. The presence of the central tower of the Cathedral rising above is another demonstration of how much it dominates the city.

Along the street of Danes Terrace can be found the county's archaeological museum, The Collection, with the Usher Gallery beyond.

The Strait

LINCOLN

P. Rooke 10

The attractive half-timbered building known as the Cardinal's Hat sits almost at the top of Lincoln's long High Street, which stretches for over a mile southwards from here (as far as St. Catherine's). Immediately to the north of the position of the viewer, the streets, which are medieval in origin, diverge from the Roman line, with the main pedestrian route being via the narrow entrance to The Strait. To the west at this point is St. Martin's Square, the site of the former church, now laid out as a garden of rest – another Lincoln Civic Trust project. As the earliest medieval coinage produced by the Lincoln mint was the St. Martin penny of c. 920, this must have been a significant early church. On its north side was the medieval hay market.

The Cardinal's Hat is named after Cardinal Wolsey, who had served successively as Dean and Bishop of Lincoln 1509-14. It was built as an inn around a courtyard. The surviving fabric, with two overhangs, dates mainly from the late 15th century, though the brick elements on the frontage belong to the 20th century. At the junction with Grantham Street (a street of 11th century origin), it incorporates part of an earlier stone structure.

Opposite, on the west side of High Street, Garmston House (Nos. 262-3) displays some characteristics of the 18th century, including its Venetian windows. From 1911, this frontage had served as the entrance to Lincoln's first 'electric cinema', but after the cinema's closure it fell into some disrepair and for over a decade was marked by scaffolding. Its restoration in the 1990s revealed part of a Norman wall along its northern side and a synagogue to its rear is attested by documents.

The Cardinal's Hat

AND UPPER HIGH STREET

P. Rooke 10

The so-called Greestone Centre (1893) is named after Greestone Stairs that lie immediately to its east, leading from Lindum Road up to Minster Yard through the site of a minor gate into the Close. ('Greestone' is derived from the Middle English for 'flight of steps'.) It was formerly the Lincoln Christ Hospital Girls' School, but is now occupied by the Art and Design department of the University of Lincoln. It forms another pleasing addition to the late Victorian townscape by the accomplished local architect William Watkins, who was entrusted with several commissions for major public structures. He was active beyond the city, for instance with Grantham Town Hall (1868), an early major project. Others noted in this book are the restoration of High Bridge and the present River Island shop further down High Street, while the former Constitutional Club (1895) at the junction of Broadgate and Silver Street cannot go unmentioned, even if it does lie empty at present.

Watkins favoured a French or Dutch Renaissance Revival 'free style'. As with several of his other buildings in the city, Greestone is of brick with terracotta dressings, with rounded arches but also some gothic influence. Its grounds lead out westwards to those of the Usher Gallery, while further up Lindum Road, beyond a recent block of apartments, is a terrace of elegant early 19th century houses. Lower down are some large detached buildings of the 1840s, formerly residences but now in public or commercial use. Across Lindum Road is the now extensive campus of Lincoln College, based partly around the former City gaol and Sessions House, and the later School of Science and Art of the 1880s (now the Gibney Building, named after the founder of the earlier School of Art in 1863). This last, another Dutch Renaissance-inspired building, was in 1902 given the status of a Day School, later known as the City School. It moved to a new site in 1968. In poor condition, in advance of its proposed demolition in the early 1970s, it was considered suitable accommodation for the city's new archaeological team, who were then subsequently moved into the adjacent and rather dank former City gaol, itself scheduled for demolition. It is pleasing to note that sense prevailed and both structures were subsequently restored, but only after the archaeologists had moved out.

The Greestone Centre

LINCOLN

P. Rooke 10

The impressive frontage of Lincoln's Drill Hall, facing on to Broadgate, is not as well appreciated as it might be, as most of those who pass it are concentrating on the busy road ahead of them. The road actually sits over the old city ditch, filled in c. 1590, while the line of the Roman city wall lay immediately behind the frontage. The wall is recorded as still standing c. 18 feet (c. 5.5m) high in the 18th century, but subsequent development removed any upstanding remains.

The new buildings along the route included the landmark of St. Swithin's church, whose spire (added in 1887) and east end (completed in 1880) are here visible. With financial support from the engineering firm Clayton and Shuttleworth, it was built to designs by the prolific church architect James Fowler. There had been no previous church at this point, which was used as the site of the cattle market, but it replaced a smaller building further west. Its huge size reflects that of the population of the parish, which stretched along the riverfront to the east, and as a result was the biggest parish church in the city in the late 19th century.

Not visible in this view, but standing immediately north of the church is the Greyfriars, a remarkable survival dating back to the 13th century and part of the city's Franciscan friary established here in 1237. After the Dissolution of the Monasteries ordered by Henry VIII, it spent most of the next 300 years as a school, before being opened as the City and County Museum in 1906. With its replacement by The Collection on Danes Terrace from 2005, it is now awaiting a new use.

Parts of the friary cloister and kitchens were found in excavations in the 1990s in advance of the rebuilding of part of the Central Library, whose new eastern frontage stands next to the Drill Hall. The attractive entrance range, first built in 1914 to the designs of Sir Reginald Blomfield, was refurbished as part of the library's rebuilding. This is entered from Free School Lane, adjacent to the new entrance to the Drill Hall added in 2004 as part of the scheme to refurbish it.

The Drill Hall itself had been built in 1890 at the expense of the local industrial magnate Joseph Ruston, proprietor of one of the city's great engineering companies. It proved useful as a hospital ward during the typhoid epidemic in 1905, when over 130 people died.

The Drill Hall and Broadgate

LINCOLN

R Rooke 10

We are here in the heart of the city centre, at a favourite meeting place for Lincolnians, an unmissable landmark. This is appropriate, because the city Council has been meeting here in the civic Guildhall for centuries – the city has had a mayor since at least 1206 – summoned by the moot bell since the 1370s.

The gateway that still stands here, largely rebuilt during the 15th century and completed in 1520, replaced an earlier gate, probably a medieval predecessor on the site of the Roman south gate. The Roman fortifications were extended to this line in the later second century, probably close to what was then the line of the River Witham. The wall itself ran along the north side of what are now Guildhall Street and Saltergate, and a fragment is occasionally open for view beneath the Royal Bank of Scotland.

The Stonebow's name, like several streets and places in the city, is derived from the Scandinavian, and means 'stone arch'. The statues on either side of the main arch represent the Annunciation, while the arms of King James I, who visited the city in 1617, are displayed above it. The present structure was restored and modified in the late 19th century, and the present clock was placed in position in 1885. The rooms to either side of the arches are let out to local shops.

The east wing formerly contained the city prison on part of the ground floor until a new gaol was built at the Sessions House.

It was rebuilt in sympathetic style and became the Town Clerk's offices. It now contains the civic insignia, including a charter of 1157 granted by Henry II, the Richard II sword presented by the King in 1387 (and offered to any monarch who subsequently visits the city) and the Lincoln Race Cup. Guided tours are provided on a regular basis.

Upstairs are the mayor's apartments as well as the Council chamber itself, containing a substantial oak table beneath an impressive oak roof.

Stonebow and Guildhall

LINCOLN

P. Rooke 10

Unlike the almost secret passages to the west of High Bridge on High Street, the riverfront to its east is marked by buildings that do acknowledge the significance of their waterfront setting. The north bank is dominated by the Waterside Shopping Centre, which opened in 1991, designed in a mixture of classical and vernacular pastiche. Some more interesting architecture, including two timber-framed structures, can be found along the riverside to the right of this view.

The development of the Waterside Centre provided an opportunity to explore the ancient riverside for the first time. The excavations revealed that the Roman river-line had lain much further back, almost on the line of Saltergate, and that the riverfront here had taken the form of a shelving hard-standing. The Roman docks had apparently been constructed downstream to the east of the walled city. Later in the Roman period, extensive dumping allowed land to be reclaimed and the riverfront advanced, and this process was renewed in the 10th century, before a major scheme in the Norman period that created a vertical waterfront. The earlier reclamation dumps were waterlogged and, as a result, organic materials were preserved so that objects of wood and leather were recovered, and samples taken of the material could be analysed for botanical and faunal remains. The artefacts included about a hundred shoes of Roman or medieval date, wooden tools including one resembling a bread shovel – of a form still used in some pizza ovens. Among the evidence of microscopic life was the wing of a cockroach! Its occurrence in the 4th century dumps makes it the earliest find of this species to date from Britain, and it also points to the presence of heated rooms, possibly for storing grain and other foodstuffs; the site also produced a huge collection of animal bones, with plentiful evidence that shoulders of beef were popular in the Roman period.

The pedestrian river bridge shown on this view was also installed at the same time as the Waterside Centre, replacing a similar structure from 1958. It now sits adjacent to the 'Empowerment' sculpture, which soars over the river, a legacy of the recent Public Sculpture initiative. This artwork was sponsored by Siemens, the city's leading engineering company, whose main base in the city lies a little further downstream. The building on the left was created in 1982 for C&A; on this side of it, but not really visible is City Square; it is used regularly as the venue for various activities including an ice-skating rink during the Christmas period.

The Riverside east of High Bridge

LINCOLN

P. Rooke 10

The High Bridge was constructed in 1160 to carry the High Street over the River Witham. The river was originally much wider, but gradual reclamation took place from the Roman period. From the time that the bridge was built, it has formed a pinch point in the river system, not accessible to wider boats. Goods had to be transferred to the boat waiting at the other side of the bridge. At one time, the bank would have been busy with commercial activity linked to river traffic.

There was a further addition to the medieval bridge at this side to carry the shops built here in c. 1600 – a unique feature in England, and still used as a shop and café/restaurant. The shops were extensively restored under the guidance of the distinguished local architect William Watkins in 1901. The eastern part of the bridge formerly carried a medieval chapel to Thomas Becket. From 1539 there was a conduit head here, provided by the City Council to dispense water. When the chapel was demolished in 1762 an obelisk replaced it, but this too has been removed: the few surviving elements were incorporated into a new obelisk at the St. Mark's shopping precinct.

The path along the northern (left) bank of the river, leading to a narrow exit out on to High Street, is known as the Glory Hole. To the left of this view, a dogleg in the path – not at first visible to the uninitiated – takes the walker past the warehouse building known as the 'Scout Hut', formerly the local scouts' headquarters. There is also a path on the south side of the river, adjacent to the northern wall of Marks and Spencer's store (1973-4) – a wall that appears never to have been given a final finish, even though it was rendered to give the impression of bays.

To the rear of this view is the path beneath Wigford Way that leads to the Brayford Pool.

High Bridge

AND THE 'GLORY HOLE' FROM THE WEST

P. Rooke 10

On most weekdays, the central commercial area between the Stonebow and St. Mary's Street is busy with shoppers. This section of High Street was the first to be pedestrianised, in 1974, and the success of the scheme here, as in other towns, has led to continual expansion of pedestrian-friendly zones. This view provides a good idea of the general 'feel' of the area. The most prominent building is the current River Island shop, yet another distinctive design by the local architect William Watkins, using terracotta produced by Doulton's of Lambeth. Some of the most unpromising buildings can conceal features of interest: for instance no. 195, a little to the north of River Island, contains an intact 15th century roof.

There are several banks in this area, which has had a long history of commercial activity. From as early as the 2nd century AD, it was developed for Roman traders' houses. Before the Roman conquest in the mid 1st century AD, it lay on an island ('River Island' is very appropriate!), between the two courses of the river. The remains of an Iron Age circular hut were found in 1972 on the island, at a site adjacent to the railway crossing.

It dated to c. 100 BC. Their two principal routes from the south meeting here, the Romans built a causeway across the more southerly river course – in the area of St. Mark's – and a bridge over the northern river. The area along High Street was reoccupied by the early 10th

St. Mary's Conduit

century, the suburb to the south of the river being known as 'Wigford'. This long suburb eventually extended all the way to St. Catherine's. It contained twelve parish churches, as well as the Carmelite friary. A little to the north of this view was the site of one of the churches, St. John, within the square known as Cornhill, the later cornmarket.

Immediately before the railway crossing is one of the city's two 11th century churches, St. Mary-le-Wigford. Its tower, added to the narrow nave, has an inscribed stone incorporated into its west wall. This stone was originally a Roman tombstone; an Anglo-Saxon inscription was inserted in the space above, recording the founder of the church, Eirtig. In front of the church is the structure known as St. Mary's Conduit, built from the remains of a friary chapel to contain a tank for the city's 16th century water-supply.

Shopping precinct,
High Street

LINCOLN

P. Rooke 10

The Brayford Pool is an essential feature of Lincoln that has been overshadowed by the prominent Cathedral. Yet it is the source of the first syllable of the city's name: the stem 'lind' was the pre-Roman British word for 'pool'. Excavations and observations, particularly since the development of a new university campus on its south bank, have demonstrated that the Pool was formerly a much greater expanse of water, and that it contained at least three large islands.

The site from where this view was taken, on the present south bank, now forms a main pedestrian route into the campus, one trodden by thousands of students each year. This was also a view of the city favoured by the landscape artists of the 18th and 19th centuries, including J. M. W. Turner. At that time, the Pool was busy with boats and boatyards, especially in the period between the reopening of the Fossdyke canal in 1744 and the coming of the railways in 1846. There are still plenty of moorings, but now for pleasure vessels. Several of the warehouses that surrounded the Pool survived until the late 20th century but, sadly, not long enough for them to be converted to fashionable residential units. Most of the office buildings that replaced them in the 1970s were of less architectural merit and largely lacked vision. Matters have improved since, and particularly with the arrival of the university, the Pool has again regained commercial vibrancy – but this time from the development of bars, restaurants and hotels.

The north bank that houses some of the new structures has also welcomed the ten-screen Odeon Cinema, a much-needed facility. As is apparent from the picture, it does steal some of the Cathedral's limelight from this perspective. Again, excavations here, and on adjacent sites, identified the reclamation deposits as the waterfront advanced from the Roman line that lay up to 100m to the east and north. This advance was, partly an 11th- and 12th century phenomenon: the suburb of Newland was created to the west of the city wall, which itself was extended to the new waterfront.

The bridge visible on the right side of the picture is for the line of Wigford Way (1971), a new road that was to be the first element of an Inner Ring Road. It did relieve the High Street of traffic and facilitated the pedestrian scheme, but the rest of the Inner Ring Road was never built. The course of the river that runs beneath the bridge is described elsewhere.

Brayford Pool

LINCOLN

P. Rooke 10

The former Great Central Warehouse, a goods depot built in 1907 that is prominent in this view, now serves as the Library of the University of Lincoln. It is an imaginative conversion, along with two other former railway buildings to the north and the south on Brayford Wharf East that also belong to the University: at the junction with Ropewalk is the former stationmaster's house, now Enterprise@ Lincoln, premises for starter businesses set up by graduates of the university. Further north, immediately south of the railway is the Engine Shed, a new structure wrapped around the original hall where steam engines were once stabled. It is used as the Students' Union building and also contains a large performance space for musical events. A Performing Arts Centre has since been added to its west side. Since much of the new campus has necessarily had to consist of new blocks, it is gratifying to see these three re-used so imaginatively. Out of view on the north side of the railway is a listed signal-box of 1873, now redundant and in need of tender loving care (which might involve a move to a heritage railway).

The disused former bridge across the river is rusting and at risk of demolition. The wide new pedestrian bridge beyond provides a welcoming entrance to that part of the campus on the south side of the railway. It includes the white Architecture Building and a Science block; new structures for other faculties are planned. These buildings connect with the rest of the Brayford campus via a bridge over the railway, with the student village beyond. This wholesale transformation of former railway land, developed at an exhilarating pace, has involved a huge amount of investment.

The University has also spread eastwards. Back across Brayford Wharf East are the former offices and printworks of the *Lincolnshire Echo* newspaper, currently under conversion to the Faculty of Business and Law, and another accommodation block at the junction with St. Mark Street. Venturing south from here leads to the St. Mark's retail park, which incorporates the restored former Midland station of 1846, earlier by two years than the current Lincoln Central. Services were concentrated at the latter when St. Mark's was closed in 1985.

St. Mark's Station

Great Central Warehouse

AND THE UNIVERSITY OF LINCOLN CAMPUS

P. Rooke 10

Although they are located in the lower part of High Street, well to the south of both the prime historic core and the pedestrianised shopping precinct, the principal buildings depicted here are two of the city's most remarkable survivals from the medieval period. They are open to the public at times, and are well worth a visit.

St. Mary's Guildhall sits over the eastern part of the Roman Fosse Way, the route to Leicester and the south-west, a little to the south of its deviation from the line of the Ermine Street that headed to London. The base of the first milestone going south was found during the excavations here. The original structure consisted of the front (west) range, most of which survives, and an east-west range later replaced. It was probably built as the town residence for King Henry II when he came to Lincoln in 1157. By the following century, the control of the building had passed to the Guild of St. Mary, the premier social organisation for the leading merchants. At the time of the Dissolution of the Monasteries, it passed to the City Council, and was subsequently used for a while as a school and as a brewery, before a rather ignominious era as a builder's yard. A restoration scheme in the 1980s by the Lincoln Civic Trust, whose offices occupy part, returned the west range to excellent condition, but the northern range, a rebuild incorporating much medieval fabric, still awaits attention. The front displays some Romanesque sculptural detail, particularly in the form of the string-course, but the interior contains more of interest as well as a section of the Roman road under glass.

St. Peter's church, beyond Sibthorp Street (a Victorian insertion), is one of the few medieval churches in the city not to have been thoroughly rebuilt (although the north aisle and chancel are of 19th century date). Its distinctive tall tower, added to an earlier nave, is of a type found at many churches in the county; they were designed to accommodate bells that featured prominently in a new form of burial service introduced by Lanfranc, the first Norman Archbishop of Canterbury, in the late 11th century. On the street in front is St. Peter's Conduit, a decorative tank-container that formed one element of the city's 16th century water supply.

There are several other buildings of interest in this particular part of High Street, which is known to have contained some very fine medieval town-houses. The suburb of Wigford, which extended southwards from the river from as early as the 10th century, had twelve parish churches in all.

St. Mary's Guildhall

AND ST. PETER AT GOWT'S CHURCH

P. Rooke 10

The former Methodist church of St. Catherine's that dominates this view lies at the very southern end of the High Street, immediately outside the two medieval gates – Bargate and Little Bargate – that defined the suburb of Wigford. It was built in 1887-8; the tower was completed twenty years later. Although it lies on the edge of the historic city, this area has produced evidence of human activity from the later Mesolithic period (c. 5000 BC) as far back as any other site. Roman cemeteries had extended this far southwards along the main streets. In the medieval period it was a busy area, containing hospitals and the important priory of St. Katherine. The area to the east was known as Swine Green, and there was a triangular-shaped market here, later truncated by the construction of the City Wall. Beyond the green was a leper hospital.

The priory was of the Gilbertine order, the only English monastic order, whose base was at Sempringham in south Lincolnshire. It was established in Lincoln from 1148 and covered an extensive area on the western side of the road, incorporating a hospital and running back to the River Witham. Little was known about the layout of the priory until the past decade, when several of the Victorian buildings along the main road (St. Catherine's) were replaced, allowing an opportunity for archaeological investigations. The location of the monastic church appears to have been identified to the south of this view, with what might have been the hospital chapel further south. Excavations near to the church revealed the green-glazed ceramic pipe that brought water to the priory. A further section of the pipe was discovered inside the church in 2009, adjacent to medieval foundations, and both are now on public display under glass inside the restored building, now a community and education centre. The water was probably brought along an aqueduct from a spring high up on South Common, where the remains of a possible cistern and pipeline course are discernible. After its closure, part of the priory was incorporated into a large residence for the prominent Grantham family, who accommodated King James I on a visit in 1617.

The eastern side of the road here was the location of the first of the Eleanor Crosses: King Edward I's wife had died at nearby Harby in 1290 when he was away. Her body was brought to the Priory where it remained overnight and was embalmed before the long journey to London. Crosses were set up at each overnight resting-place. The only remains of the Lincoln example, badly damaged during the Civil War in 1648, are preserved at the Castle.

St. Catherine's

LINCOLN

P. Rooke. 10

This view looking towards the Cathedral from the lower slopes of South Common provides an informative setting for the situation of the historic walled town. The Cathedral and Castle sit atop the northern scarp of the Witham Gap, while South Common occupies a good part of the southern scarp. To the west (left) of this view, the line of the High Street and the suburb of Wigford extend as far St. Catherine's at the edge of the Common.

Now a valuable green space and largely wild area of grasses that is much appreciated by the local populace, and used for casual recreational purposes, the Common has seen much activity over the centuries. A survey of the remaining earthworks – humps and bumps – was undertaken in 2003 by specialist fieldworkers from English Heritage as part of a national project on urban commons. In spite of the difficulties of identifying earlier remains caused by landscaping for a golf course and for cricket and football pitches, they revealed a great number of archaeological features.

The earliest of these was a cambered section of the line of the Ermine Street, the main Roman road between Lincoln and London. Its discovery helps to explain the context of discoveries of Roman cremations, and the tombstone of Gaius Valerius, the standard bearer of the Ninth Legion (on display in the local museum, The Collection) found in 1909. The inscribed stone might already have been displaced by the nearby excavations for the railway cutting in the 1860s. Some of the earthworks are explained as quarrying activity, for sand, clay and stone, possibly from as early as the Roman period, but certainly by the Middle Ages, when this land was used by St. Katherine's Priory. There are indications of a possible cistern high up on the Common and the line of an aqueduct along its northern side, which could both have served the Priory. At a later date, the land was held in Common, that is, local citizens had rights of pasture.

Other remains noted included butts for rifle practice – a favourite pastime for some in the Victorian era, and First World War practice trenches. The prototype tanks invented and developed at Foster's Works were also tested here in 1915. The two ornamental ponds were probably developed from existing quarry-pits.

South Common

LINCOLN

P. Rooke 10

The approach to Lincoln from the west, along the A57 and past the former racecourse, is an attractive entrance-way to the city. Visible on the skyline in addition to the Cathedral is Ellis' Mill, the last of a row of windmills on the ridge to survive. West Common, a large expanse of open grassland, is an amenity highly valued by the community, in particular those people who live close to it in the west end. It was formerly dominated by Lincoln Racecourse, including the surviving grandstand building, but in spite of the course's closure in 1964 it still fulfils a community function.

It has witnessed some varied and special uses in its time. In the 3rd century AD there were Roman pottery kilns on the south-west side of the present Saxilby Road. The common fields as such could have been in use from before the Norman Conquest, possibly then extending to the city walls. Ridge and furrow earthworks are still visible across most of the common, while on the lower, flatter ground there are indications of early quarrying, much obscured by the landscaping operations for the golf course.

The racecourse – initially in a simple form – came here in 1773, and a properly graded course was created from 1826. The straight mile was the course for the Lincolnshire Handicap, the first 'classic' of the flat racing season. A grandstand was provided, both to provide a clear view and for its social value, and in due course was replaced by larger structures; only that of 1897 survives. Meetings were occasional, and there was plenty of op-

portunity to accommodate other events and activities. A swimming pool was built close to the Fossdyke Canal in 1874, with a smallpox hospital nearby! Lincoln Golf Club had a course created on the lower ground from 1891; after the typhoid epidemic of 1905, when the hospital was used as an isolation ward, the course was taken over in 1906 by the Carholme Golf Club, but its extent had, at times, to be curtailed for other events. In June 1907 (and in 1947) the Royal Show was held here. A special pavilion was erected for King Edward VII's use, and the pond was re-landscaped for the occasion. It attracted 133,026 paying visitors over its five days. Within less than a decade, war conditions dictated that the common was used both as a practice ground for digging trenches and as an aircraft acceptance park, where some of the aeroplanes built in Lincoln were tested. Hangars were constructed for Sopwith Camels and Handley Page bombers. One runway was a chalk circle 250m in diameter.

West Common

LINCOLN

P. Rooke 10

What had been a largely open space on the hillside to the north of Monks Road was opened in 1872 as the city's Arboretum, the idea being to provide 'innocent enjoyment' for the working classes, both local and visitors. The land here had formerly been part of the extensive Monks Leys estate, at one time associated with the small priory (Monks Abbey) whose fragmentary remains still survive a little further east.

Having been unable to obtain permission from the Dean and Chapter for a similar scheme on the north side of Yarborough Road, the city Corporation again engaged the accomplished landscape gardener Edward Milner to design the park, with a requirement for particular elements. The costs spiralled to the then significant sum of £7500, in spite of some exhibits being donated. These included the lion, made of coade-stone, given by the mayor Francis Clarke, who grew wealthy from sales of his 'Blood Mixture', a potion widely believed to cure all sorts of illness. The official opening in August 1872 was a well-publicised and well-attended event, and crowds estimated at 10,000 included many who had travelled by train from outside the city. A fee was charged for entrance. The upper terrace, 300 metres long, was graced by lime trees and a glass pavilion; the pavilion is no longer standing.

Having been successfully established, further improvements were made. The bandstand shown in this view, which is portrayed from adjacent to the lodge and main gate, was a gift in 1884 from The Manchester Unity of Oddfellows, a 'friendly society' whose bands played here. The fountain in the lake was provided to mark the arrival of Lincoln's new water supply in 1911, a belated response by the Corporation, chastened by the typhoid epidemic of 1905.

The Arboretum sits on the hillside above the working class housing erected in terraces off the south side of Monks Road to accommodate the growing numbers needed in the factories across the river. On its north side, in contrast, are several large villas which sit on a strip of land that was sold to help pay for the costs of the park.

As part of a national scheme to restore historic gardens, a grant was obtained from the Heritage Lottery Fund in 2003 to help refurbish the park and the structures within it. It is now in good condition and invites wider appreciation.

The Arboretum

LINCOLN

P. Rooke 10

The first bridge across the River Witham downstream from Lincoln is the spot from which this view back to the city is depicted. It is known as the Five-Mile Bridge, a little to the east of the village of Fiskerton, whose church can be seen above the trees, centre-right. To the left, the Cathedral towers are clearly discernible; on a clear day they can be seen from the edge of the Wolds, about 20 miles east of the city.

The Witham hereabouts is a peaceful sort of river, wider than its canalised course through the city. It can best be appreciated by taking a boat, or from the Water Rail Way, a riverside cycle path. The path lies over the course of the former Lincoln-Bardney-Kirkstead railway, and is ultimately to be extended all the way to Boston. It is notable for the artworks with local themes along the route.

In the prehistoric period, the river was much wider with a winding course, and not far to the east of here the remains of an estuarine creek system for an earlier course have been detected. There is an increasing amount of evidence to suggest that this stretch of the valley was part of a 'ritual' landscape from at least as early as the Bronze Age (from c. 2500 BC). Concentrations of round barrows (circular burial mounds) have been found on both sides of the river at several locations east of Lincoln. These may have been at least partly submerged as water levels rose subsequently and deposits of peat accumulated along the valley. By the Later Bronze Age (c. 1200-7000 BC), causeways were being constructed across wet ground adjacent to the main channel at key points, the best-known example being that excavated in 1981 on the east side of Fiskerton, not far from this viewpoint. It was probably at or adjacent to the causeways that precious metal objects were placed in the river, or in pools or meres close to it, as votive offerings. Some of the finest prehistoric metalwork from Britain, including the Witham Shield (Iron Age, c. 300 BC), was found in the river during improvement works in the late 18th and early 19th centuries. The valley has also produced some remarkable artefacts from later periods. The finds from Fiskerton include many metal artefacts and a log-boat, and are on display at The Collection in Lincoln.

Five-Mile View

LINCOLN

P. Rooke 10

The Story of Lincoln

With a past as rich and complex as that of any town in Britain, Lincoln is a jewel for enthusiasts of history, architecture and archaeology. Its situation, at a gap in the Jurassic limestone ridge, has been perceived as a special one since before the Roman conquest. The gap, where the Rivers Till and Witham met, was then and still is a distinctive feature in the landscape. On a clear day it can be best appreciated from miles away to the east.

In this brief account, we can hardly do justice to the city's historical wealth, but I hope that along with the commentaries on Peter Rooke's paintings the essence of such a special place will emerge. Neither the written text nor the paintings are, however, a real substitute for experiencing its historic attractions at first hand. These do not all lie in the historic centre; as should be apparent from the images, there is much of interest below hill and on the fringes. Not only is Lincoln a cathedral city, but for over a century it has also been a major centre of heavy engineering, with some firms achieving world renown. The service industries have become increasingly important with the decline in manufacturing, and an important element in this has been the creation of a still expanding university by the Brayford Pool. Its establishment since 1996 has provided a major stimulus.

ORIGINS

The area that has undergone the most radical change in the past decade – the university by the Brayford Pool – is also that which has produced the first evidence for Lincoln's earliest human occupants. Sampling of deposits on what were, in the later Mesolithic Period (about 5000 BC), islands in the much larger pool or sandy banks adjacent to the river, has yielded evidence of flint tool manufacture. The presence of cemeteries from the Bronze Age – over 3000 years later – in the form of round barrows (burial mounds) has been established at several points downstream, the nearest only a mile or so east of the city. The Witham Valley hereabouts appears to have been a focus of ritual activity, with offerings made into the river of precious metal artefacts from the Later Bronze Age. This phenomenon appears to have continued into later periods.

For the Iron Age tribe (the Corieltavi) occupying this region immediately before the Roman conquest, Lincoln's natural situation may already have been important, not only for particular rituals, but also as a crossing-point. The earliest definite settlement belongs to the first century BC: in 1972, traces were uncovered of timber houses and contemporary pottery on what was then an island in the Pool. Pre-Roman activity might have been expected: the first syllable of the Roman name Lindum is derived from the Celtic word for 'pool' or 'lake'.

THE ROMAN ARRIVAL

During the mid 1st century AD, Lincoln became for the first time a major centre of population, with the arrival of a Roman legion and construction of its fortress. The army appreciated the strategic advantages afforded by the gap in the ridge that allowed transportation by river and control of native movements. The fortress was built, in timber, on top of the hill to accommodate the Ninth Legion, whose soldiers originated from provinces close to the Mediterranean. Excavations along the line of the walls of the city that succeeded it confirmed that the fortifications of the legionary fortress lay directly beneath. The legionary headquarters, the principia, was discovered in 1978-79 beneath the civic forum. Few of the other buildings, including the many barracks, have been investigated. Other areas were required outside the base for traders, supplies and burial grounds, and the legionary occupation must have taken over a large area of land. The feelings of the native people are not recorded but the arrival of so many military men from abroad would have been a traumatic event for them. At the same time, it offered some opportunities: the invaders required vast quantities of food, equipment and building materials, and only some of these could have been transported with them.

COLONY

The legionary presence at Lincoln did not last more than 20-30 years. After this period the tribal area of the Corieltavi was sufficiently pacified for the military zone to be moved northwards and westwards. The Ninth left in AD 71 to build York; the Second Adiutrix that replaced it had moved to found Chester by AD 79. The army had not only built an internally-planned and defended enclosure; it had also required the construction of major roads from the south and south-west, respectively the Ermine Street (now partly the A15) and the Fosse Way (now the A46). The expedient decision was now made to take advantage of the existing infrastructure by establishing a colonia, a self-governing community of retired soldiers, on the site of the former fortress. On retirement, the legionaries were given grants of money and land, and were encouraged to develop a city on the Roman model. The exact date at which Lindum Colonia came into existence is unknown: it was certainly before AD 96, on the basis of an inscription found at Mainz in Germany. The city grew to become a cosmopolitan and prosperous place, with visitors and new residents arriving from various parts of the empire.

In order to be a recognisable Roman city, the authorities and leading citizens first had to invest in a major programme of public works over the next few decades. The fortifications were provided with a stone front, and new street-surfaces were laid down over a system of drains. The spiritual, legal and administrative centre was the forum, normally found also at the physical heart. At Lincoln, it was erected on the site of the former legionary headquarters, and initially took the form of an open precinct containing some official statues, including that of

the emperor, and probably a state temple. Subsequently, by the early 3rd century, a town hall (basilica) was erected on the north side of the central courtyard, which was otherwise surrounded by double ranges of rooms. Porticoed walkways overlooked the central piazza, and a magnificent row of 19 columns, including two entrances, provided an impressive frontage on to the main street of the city. Some of the rooms in the street-frontage were reserved for traders and craftsmen undertaking repairs, but the larger commercial and industrial establishments were located outside the walls.

Part of the excavated east range of the forum, including a well, is now on public display, as is the nearby 'Mint Wall', an impressive section of the north wall of the civic basilica. The public baths lay to the north and east of the principal street, and conveniently close to the Roman water-reservoir on the northern defences. An aqueduct supplied this tank, tapping a source at least 2 km to the north-east, but its workings are still imperfectly understood. There must also have been other temples and a theatre, still awaiting discovery. Much of the land to the rear of the two main streets was occupied by the houses of the local aristocracy which became increasingly well appointed as time went on.

The hillside below the fortress was occupied initially by commercial traders. It was also provided with a street-grid as far as the gradient would allow: the main route up the steepest part was engineered in steps and ramps, while wheeled vehicles had to take a zig-zag detour. Apart from the main street itself, which was lined with public buildings including an octagonal public fountain, these south-facing slopes were largely given over to aristocratic residences; the displaced traders now lined the suburban streets. The fortifications were extended to include the hillside settlement, almost as far down as the river.

There was also extensive development beyond the walls. The riverside was a focus of trading activity, including shelving beaches on which to draw up river-craft. The river at this time was much wider than now, and gradual reclamation was necessary partly because its level was rising. Where the Waterside Shopping Centre now stands, a series of inlets and artificial piers was discovered (the docks were downstream of this point). Those excavations also produced vast amounts of well-preserved artefacts, including large numbers in organic materials: for instance, leather shoes, a wooden bread shovel, and part of a Roman writing-tablet. The huge dumps of butchers' waste used for land reclamation were notable for the abundance of shoulders of beef, a popular cut of meat.

Beyond the river and to the south lay the most extensive suburb, largely taken up with commercial properties of long narrow buildings, closely set, which had shops on their street frontages. These extended for almost a kilometre. They supplied a variety of products, from foodstuffs to metalwork, to the local populace. Similar properties have also been found outside other gates of the city, while most of the cemeteries lay beyond them. Further out were industrial concerns which supplied the city's needs, including sand and gravel workings, stone quarries and pottery kilns.

PROVINCIAL CAPITAL

When Britain was subdivided into four at the end of the third century, Lincoln's status and success may have influenced its choice to be provincial capital; as such, it also became a bishopric from AD 313. The presence in the city of new government officials – the military bureaucracy – meant an injection of spending power and some employment for local people.

One consequence of Lincoln's important role in the imperial system was a costly and time-consuming strengthening of the fortifications, a contemporary symbol of the city's new status. The city wall was thickened internally or completely rebuilt to a width of 3-4 m, in places incorporating re-used fragments from earlier monuments – a further indication of the change in priorities. A much larger ditch was now created, in keeping with late Roman defensive strategy. The impact was to create a defensive barrier which survived for centuries and influenced the layout of the town for even longer.

Money was still being lavished on aristocratic town houses – the local elite were investing in their rural villas too – but little in the way of public building was taking place apart from that on the city walls. The most remarkable residence, palatial in scale, was the so-called 'Greetwell villa' which overlooked the Witham valley to the east of the city, and was possibly the base of the provincial governor.

This prestigious era all came to an end in a matter of decades. By the end of the 4th century, there was extensive – but not complete – desertion of the urban area. The survivors may possibly have formed a small self-sufficient community practising agriculture and horticulture and keeping animals within the walls. It also appears that buildings were still being erected, but in timber rather than stone.

Britons, Anglo-Saxons and Danes

In the almost complete absence of historical sources and limited archaeological evidence, a coherent narrative for the next few centuries is difficult. The former Roman city suffered along with all others in the collapse of the imperial system in Britain in the early 5th century. Lincoln had ceased to be a town before the Anglo-Saxon takeover of Eastern England, but the remnants of the Romano-British population may have retained control of the Lincoln area for another century or so. They had the use of a well-fortified area with good road and river communications, and an association with a once mighty empire which provided a symbolic base for a new political leader, whether a bishop or a warlord. Yet the streets were not maintained and buildings became ruinous, and both gradually fell into disuse. At some point a timber church was erected on the forum courtyard, related architecturally to the western portico, and possibly making use of the well in the east range as a baptistery. It was built no earlier than the late 4th century, and radiocarbon analysis of subsequent graves suggests that it had probably been demolished by AD 600. It is possible that it was built as a symbolic act, to help legitimise the ruler of the sub-Roman community and reinforce the link back to the Roman Empire.

The Anglo-Saxons brought with them a building tradition in timber, a pagan religion, and a society and an economy in which towns on the Roman model had no place. Archaeological finds suggest that the area of the former Roman province controlled by Lincoln was in due course penetrated by Angles (from the Jutland peninsula), and that to the south (whose capital had been at London) by Saxons. Lincoln was, or became, a major political centre in the kingdom of Lindsey, although lying on its southern boundary. Bede wrote of the events of c. 627-8 when Bishop Paulinus came to Lincoln from York, and converted Blecca, described as *prefect of the city* – perhaps the king's representative – and his household. Paulinus built a stone church *of remarkable workmanship*. This church used for the consecration of Honorius, the fifth Archbishop of Canterbury, has not yet been found. Could it have involved a re-use and modification of the Roman town hall (basilica)?

Burial, perhaps restricted to an aristocratic group, continued without a break within the former forum courtyard. One grave contained a bronze hanging-bowl – possibly tableware for the social elite – dating to the seventh century, with fine decorative attachments (it is now on display in the Cathedral Treasury). These 'escutcheons' were excellent examples of contemporary British craftsmanship. The fact that Lincolnshire has now produced so many objects of this type reinforces the idea of continuing British influence. The single-celled structure containing the grave here subsequently became the original core of a parish church which survived, after many rebuildings, until 1971.

Apart from this church site, the Anglo-Saxon settlement may also have contained a number of other Christian foci. One appears to have been located immediately inside the lower walled town north of the Stonebow, where 8th-9th century graves were discovered in excavations east of the former site of St. Peter-at-Arches. Nearby to the north was another St. Peter's church: it is conceivable that both had originally formed part of a monastic establishment or cathedral, sited here to make use of the adjacent Roman public fountain as a baptistery.

The former Roman city may have been characterised by a series of farmsteads. This is one possible explanation for the concentration of finds of 9th century pottery in the grounds of the Lawn, west of the Castle; but there are other interpreta-tions as a market, or a nearby high-status residence. Only in the past year or so has Lincoln produced evidence for a mid-Saxon riverside trading settlement outside the Roman walls (a wic, from the Latin *vicus*). As with similar settlements at London and York, the finds of 7th- and 8th century pottery were made at a site on the fringe of the former city. At the time it was probably another island (later 'Thorngate Island'), lying to the south of the river channel and to the south-east of the walled city.

The Danish Commercial Impetus

Before the end of the ninth century, Danish settlement had begun and within a century Lincoln became the largest of the 'Five Boroughs' of the East Midlands ('Danish Mercia'). Again, the Roman fortified enclosure and the surviving communications were surely important factors in the choice of the site. Lincoln resumed its status as a commercial and trading hub. The economies of York and Lincoln were growing quickly during the tenth century, and Danish trading activity contributed significantly to this growth. A mint was established, and the number of moneyers making coins indicates that Lincoln rivalled York for second place after London. Their names suggest that, unlike York, Lincoln's population contained as many English as Scandinavians.

Archaeological excavations have allowed us to elucidate the pattern of growth and new planning over the next two centuries, with the earliest occupation beginning in the lower walled city, north of the River Witham. New suburbs were established to the east and south, but the upper city may have remained a royal preserve for a little longer. Further parts of the lower city and the eastern suburb of Butwerk also seem to have been occupied before 1066.

Only in excavations since the 1970s have the slight traces of occupation in this period been recognised. They included remains of both houses and workshops in an industrial quarter at the junction of Grantham Street and Flaxengate. A sequence was identified of about thirteen periods of timber construction between c. 880 and c. 1230, when the first stone building was erected here – an average life of about twenty-five years. Most of the walls were probably constructed of horizontally-laid planks, their roofs of thatch. Another type of structure included a semi-basement, often created out of surviving Roman masonry and used primarily for storage purposes.

A new cobbled street was laid out in about AD 900 parallel to the Roman Ermine Street, probably the first re-planning since the second century. This lane was known as 'Haraldstigh' (and only centuries later renamed Flaxengate). About a century or so later, an east-west street ('Brancegate', now Grantham Street) was constructed to link the two. Workshops and nearby rubbish layers and pits contained many fragments of evidence for industrial activity: spinning, working in jet, bone and antler (including combs), and metallurgical activity including copper alloy and silver. Items such as finger rings were made of glass and copper alloy (some from recycling Roman objects). At nearby Silver Street, production of pottery tempered with fragments of shell began in the late ninth century; later kiln-sites have since turned up along Pottergate ('the street of the potters'), which emerged from the lower east gate and ran up the hillside.

Excavation of waterlogged deposits close to the river has produced shoes and other leather and wooden objects, together with evidence for diet and for the local environment. A rare silk scarf of Byzantine origin was discovered in 1973 in damp deposits at Silver Street, similar enough to be part of the same roll also used for a scarf found at York a few years later. In the 10th century, new waterfronts were being constructed against the river. They were timber structures designed for small rivercraft; part of a hull of a clinker-built boat was incorporated into a later wharf or jetty.

The vast majority of the medieval city's forty-seven parish churches were in existence by 1100. Many appear to have been established from the later tenth century. The church of St. Paul-in-the-Bail, so significant earlier, now became merely another parish church. St. Mark in Wigford, the only other church to have been completely excavated, appears to have originated in the mid to late 10th century as a small timber structure with an adjacent graveyard. Another in existence in the 10th century was St. Martin which stood at the top of upper High Street. It is also presumed that an early Minster lay beneath or near to the present Cathedral. The churchyards were used for markets in this period. Stone architecture was introduced for the churches from the 11th century, but the domestic building tradition was still in timber.

By 1066, then, Lincoln was a growing town with a population of perhaps 5-8,000, in the second rank along with Norwich, Winchester and York. The upper city contained many houses, but the lower part of town functioned as the municipal and commercial centre. The Scandinavians had introduced an early form of local government, their twelve 'lawmen' being the predecessor of the medieval council, and the subsequent introduction of earldoms by King Cnut heralded the creation of the shire.

The Norman City: Castle And Cathedral

After absorbing the shock of the Norman Conquest, Lincoln's prosperity increased further for another two centuries, only to decline subsequently. Within a few years, work had begun on creating the two great monuments of the medieval city. William returned southwards via Lincoln after his first campaign in the North, and in 1068 ordered a castle to be built. With a hilltop enclosure at his disposal, he was already provided with a symbol of the might of a previous empire, and he made expedient use of the upper Roman enclosure, strengthening its gates. It was the next century before a smaller castle was carved out of the south-western quarter of this enclosure. The rest of the upper Roman city then became the Castle's outer bailey – the Bail – and, like the Cathedral Close, did not legally become part of the city proper again until 1836.

The Castle was the scene of three notable military events. The first in 1141 occurred as a result of the dispute between supporters of Stephen and those of his cousin, the Empress Matilda, who was championed by Ranulf, Earl of Chester. Stephen was imprisoned, but was back in control again by Christmas 1146. Another struggle followed in 1216 after the then Constable, Nicholaa de la Haye, would not relinquish control to supporters of Louis of France. The English king's army recaptured the city in the following year, before pillaging the town for having supported the opposition. There was further action in the English Civil War of 1644-8, when Parliamentary troops had little difficulty in storming it.

In subsequent centuries, the Castle's functions have been primarily as a seat of local government, and to dispense law and order. The walls and gates, even though much repaired, still contain a great deal of interest. There were two mottes. In the south-western corner is the original or 'Lucy's Tower', surmounted by stone walls probably added in the mid-12th century. At the south-eastern angle is a mid-12th century tower, considered to have been originally the work of Ranulf in the struggles of the 1140s mentioned above. At the north-eastern corner lies the 13th century Cobb Hall, containing remains of an early gaol in its basement.

The main entrance from Castle Hill, the East Gate, belongs, like Cobb Hall, mainly to the first half of the 13th century, having been damaged in the battle of 1217. In its heyday it was an impressive structure, but its external barbican towers no longer survive above modern ground-level. The West Gate, in contrast, only re-opened in 1993, is largely of 12th century date, but again with strengthening, including a portcullis dated to 1233-4. Immediately north of the Norman gate was its Roman equivalent, suddenly revealed in 1836 when the landlord of the adjacent Strugglers Inn was attempting to extend his garden by removing the base of the castle bank. The Roman arch had to be reburied after it collapsed forward.

The Cathedral

William rewarded another Norman supporter, Remigius, from the abbey of Fécamp, with the bishopric in 1067. It became the centre of the largest diocese in England, extending beyond Oxford. By the date of Remigius' death in 1092, his cathedral was only days away from consecration. This consisted primarily of a free-standing tower, probably built to the west of an existing major Anglo-Saxon minster. Its function was partly to provide accommodation for the bishop, who, as a knight, had military responsibilities. In other words, it was the original keep or great tower of the first castle.

Lincoln Cathedral is treasured by the local community and by many who visit the city. Its architectural beauty, and its scale, enhanced by its hilltop position, have drawn many favourable comments, such as those of the 19th century critic John Ruskin:

> '… the Cathedral at Lincoln is out and out the most precious piece of architecture in the British Isles and, roughly speaking, worth any two other Cathedrals we have'.

It is a vast and complex structure containing work and styles of several different ages, although its principal elements are Early English Gothic, with some later additions and changes. Significant Norman elements surviving at the west end include original niches and the remarkable frieze commissioned by Bishop Alexander in the second quarter of the 12th century, showing scenes from the Old and New Testaments.

A reported 'earthquake' that split it asunder in 1184 necessitated its rebuilding. What resulted became the greatest surviving example of Early English Gothic architecture. The new building, with pointed arches, rib vaults and large windows, began under the direction of one of Lincoln's most revered bishops, Hugh of Avalon (1186-1200), funded partly by contributions from local peasants. It took the next century to complete; only the choir and the east transepts were in place by the time of Hugh's death in 1200. The main transepts and their windows followed, and the Chapter House during the 1220s. The Cathedral had been almost completely rebuilt by the time of the collapse of the central tower in 1237. A re-designed central tower, with its tall spire, was finished early in the next century, making it for the next two centuries, the tallest building in the world at 180 metres high. The nave had followed by about 1250, and the 'Angel Choir' to its east by 1280; this had involved demolishing more of the Roman fortifications, but the space created allowed for a new shrine for St. Hugh, a place of pilgrimage. Additional elements included the Cloister (c. 1300), towers, the new window in the south transept (the 'Bishop's Eye') and a new window in the west front. Several chantries date from the 15th and 16th centuries.

The Community in the Close

The medieval bishop was the wealthiest person in the city, but he had a duty to help his canons find houses for themselves, as well as for himself. Initially he also had a mansion to the west of the Castle. Bishop Alexander was provided with apartments above the East Gate, but in 1135-8 King Stephen granted him some land south of the Cathedral to create a palace. Bishop Chesney had completed its first phase by 1163, and it was further developed by Bishop Hugh of Avalon and by his successor Bishop Hugh of Wells (1209-35). As the household in-creased in size and as architectural and living styles changed, the Bishop sought to maintain his status, and the Palace was modified accordingly. Bishop Henry Burghersh had the walls crenellated in the early 13th century in line with fashion and the style of the Close Wall. The other major phase belonged to the mid-15th century, when Bishop William Alnwick created domestic arrangements for himself in contemporary style. The Palace was damaged at the time of the Lincolnshire Rising (1536) and again during the Civil War, after which it was no longer habitable.

Remigius had created a chapter of twenty-one canons, doubled by his successor. Their residences lay in Minster Yard and to its east and north, including a house for the choristers next to what became that of the Chancellor in 1321. It was among this community that scholarship flourished. Properties were gradually purchased and some bequeathed, so that by about 1300 there were sufficient for all canons in residence. There were complaints after the building of the Angel Choir had removed part of the city wall that criminals transgressed nightly and that muggings and burglaries were commonplace – and perhaps some concern to keep the clergy away from the temptations of the city! Edward I agreed to grant a licence in 1285 allowing the construction of a protective wall with towers, with gates locked overnight. The Close Wall took several decades to complete. It enclosed land well to the east of the existing walled city as well as part of it. Among its impressive entrances to survive is Exchequergate, the inner of a double gate.

The houses that also survive in the Close are some of the most attractive and historic in the city. Vicars Court is today one of its most attractive settings, but has a very different layout from its medieval form, except on part of the south side. Of particular note is the Chancery (no. 11 Minster Yard), partly for its association with Katherine Swynford, the mistress and later wife of John of Gaunt, the Duke of Lancaster and father of the future King Henry IV.

The Medieval City

The Norman arrival both disrupted and gave a fillip to the economy of the city. By 1100 Lincoln was thriving again, and soon amongst the most wealthy cities in England. Henry II's agreement to a Charter in 1157, and his wearing of the Crown that Christmas in his palace in the city, confirmed Lincoln's prominent place on the national scene. Central to the economic success were the cloth industry and wool trade, which operated on an international scale, working through Flemish merchants. Good communications were essential: the clearing out of the Fossdyke in 1121 had allowed wool from the Midlands to be transported to Lincoln via the Trent and Fossdyke, thence along the Witham to Boston and to France and Flanders. The weavers made 'Lincoln' cloth, especially its fine dyed 'scarlet', but also woollen cloth in (off-)white, grey and green. The industry was based mainly in the lower walled city, west of the High Street. Within a century or so, however, reduced demand from abroad and Flemish competition provided a challenge to which the local merchants were unable to rise and, as a result, Lincoln's economy was seriously damaged. The city could still export local wool but this was in no way as economically beneficial as the presence of manufacturing; many others depended on the weavers.

The breakdown of Lincoln's international cloth trade is mirrored by a change in pottery types in the later 13th century. The city had already had a tradition of producing most of its own pottery, but now a rural pottery industry developed and a rival centre of production grew up in Nottingham. Pottery and tile manufacture in the city moved to the southern suburb of Wigford. Other trades, some of which established guilds, included metalworkers, plumbers, locksmiths, farriers and goldsmiths. Close to the river were fishing and related activities. A prominent group of merchants founded St. Mary's Guild, the premier fraternity, or socio-religious organisation, in the city from 1251. It met in St. Mary's Guildhall in lower High Street, a palatial building that may have originated as Henry II's residence from the time of his visit in 1157.

The leading merchants were still the most prominent element of the community to engage in local government. The

Council itself contained twenty-four members, half of higher status; these were the aldermen. Lincoln obtained permission to elect a mayor, one of the first in England. The first mayor documented, Adam, was definitely in post by 1210, and sided with the Barons against King John. In 1387, Richard II granted Lincoln's mayor the right to have a sword carried before him: it is still used for ceremonial purposes when the monarch visits. It was 1422 before the City's first Constitution was confirmed, setting out that there should be a 'commonalty' or general body of the twenty-four existing 'councillors', plus another forty members. Control remained with the mayor and his inner circle of twelve.

PHYSICAL GROWTH

Many of the streets created during the Anglo-Scandinavian period continued in use; others were laid out to link them. Some were swept away by subsequent developments, including the building of the Castle. Lincoln grew in all directions, as well as becoming more built up internally. The mature medieval settlement extended in a north-south direction for about 3km. At about the time of the Norman Conquest, the various markets were moved from their previous locations in churchyards to the two main routes up the hill. The fish market lay at the junction next to the Norman House near the top of Steep Hill, the poultry market on the hill below, the corn-market just above the Jew's House. The skin and cloth markets were on the next street to the west. Fairs were also held.

New vertical timber waterfronts were developed, advancing the riverfront to a point not far from the present line. The extension of the city wall to the river, where it terminated in towers, was probably not complete until the 14th century. The western tower, later known confusingly as the Lucy Tower (the same name as the castle motte), was faced in fine ashlar. Outside the wall here, the area to the north of the Pool was part of the suburb of Newland, in existence by the 12th century; it contained a market-place. There was another riverside suburb at Thorngate, south of the river and east of High Bridge. The bridge itself dates to c.1160: its Norman structure still survives with later additions. Its construction proved a major obstacle to the passage of large vessels, so that goods had to be trans-shipped. The northern suburb, Newport, took the form of an elongated market-place, and had its own market adjacent to one of its only two churches, St. John's. These later suburbs are distinguished by the larger size of their parishes.

In addition to the Close Wall and the extensions to the river, new fortifications were constructed at the approaches to the two suburbs of Wigford and Newport. The wall and two linked Bargates built at the southern limit of Wigford were probably in place by 1217, for repairs were needed to them after the battle of that year, but surviving depictions hint at 13th century designs. A grant of 'murage' in 1322 was a royal indication that maintenance of the city walls was considered vital to protect 'the King's city'. By the time that these fortifications were complete, Lincoln had entered a long period of decline.

At the edge of the city were both fields and pastures, lying north of the Fossdyke and Witham in a wide semicircle. Towards the eastern limit, a little north of the river, a cell of the Benedictine Abbey of St. Mary of York was established within half a century of the Conquest. The southern entrances to the city were marked by several medieval establishments. The Malandry, or hospital of the Holy Innocents, was the earliest foundation, possibly by 1100. Across the street and market-place was the hospital of the Holy Sepulchre, and adjacent to it from 1148 was St. Katherine's Priory. The priory eventually covered a huge area, as well as owning considerable estates, and was active in producing wool. It belonged to the only monastic order of English origin, the Gilbertines, whose founder's principal seat was at Sempringham in Kesteven.

The urban friaries appeared in the 13th century. The Franciscans arrived in 1231 and were given land in the south-eastern corner of the walled city. Their precinct extended as far north as Silver Street. Remains of their later church were excavated nearby in 1973, while parts of the cloister and the kitchen block were revealed during rebuilding of the Central Library in 1994. The 'Greyfriars' building further south might have been the original church. The Dominicans, established in 1238, occupied a large area to the east of the lower city.

Excavations in 2003 revealed a substantial 13th century structure thought to be a claustral building, and other remains to the west. The Carmelites (White Friars) were based in Wigford by 1269. Remains of their church were discovered directly beneath the St. Mark's Railway station building, on the south side of a cloister. The Austin Friars founded a base in Newport before 1280. The Friars of the Sack established themselves at the south-eastern edge of Butwerk, close to the river. They had apparently departed by c. 1300, but the other friaries were still expanding in the 14th century.

Few new parish churches were built after c. 1100. From the 12th century it was not such a simple process to create a new parish. In any case, there were already more churches than the medieval town could sustain. Church plans developed along similar lines. In particular, the common cellular-linear Norman plan was often embellished with a west tower and the nave later widened in the Early English style. An increase in size was necessary to cope with the growing population, but was also necessitated by the changing, more elaborate liturgy: chancels were commonly extended and chapels added.

MEDIEVAL HOUSING

The earliest medieval stone residence in the city is also the most famous 12th century house in England, the Jew's House at the bottom of Steep Hill. It was certainly occupied by a Jewish merchant from the time of its construction in 1150-

60. Lincoln's other Norman house, close to the top of the hill, may have been built a few decades later. These first stone houses may have been exceptional and confined to those with both the resources and the need to keep them secure. Stone became more common in the 13th century; it was more fire-proof. The change might also be seen as a reflection of the increasing wealth of the urban community.

The Jews served as bankers of the day, facilitating investment by lending money. They had enjoyed the protection of Henry II until his death in 1189, but the Crusades provided a pretext for attacks on them. The Jews suffered again in the mid-13th century, and in 1255 Lincoln was the scene of an alleged ritual murder of a young boy ('Little St. Hugh'), a fabricated story which also appeared in several other countries. In 1290, after further persecution, the Jews were expelled from England until readmitted by Oliver Cromwell.

Decline

By the late 13th century Lincoln was in decline and the principal causes were economic. It had also been marginalised in terms of land transport by the building of the Great North Road through Newark. The general impression of the next two centuries is of abandonment and demolition of properties – especially those away from the principal route-ways. By the 15th century it was even proving difficult to find tenants for all the properties in the Close and some were demolished.

Parliament had met in the Cathedral in January 1301. While in the city Edward I granted a petition from the city for a new Charter restoring liberties that had been forfeited in 1290. The city was also granted the right to levy taxes for six years to repair roads. Matters were not helped by the Black Death of 1349. Its impact on the population was devastating: about 60% of the clergy of the city perished. In 1365, Edward III complained about physical conditions in the city and the effect they were having on trade. The King ordered the city to clean itself up and pave the streets within a year. Another blow followed. Lincoln had been one of the staple towns created in 1326 through which all goods of certain materials, including wool and hides, had to pass. That privilege was removed to Boston in 1369 which, for a few decades, eclipsed Lincoln before it too suffered a decline.

A survey of 1428 provides an impression of the decline in population. Four parishes had no inhabitants, while seventeen others contained no more than ten persons. Twelve were closed during the 15th century. Some of their former fabric was subsequently re-used, much of it incorporated into the monastic establishments. The guildhall by the south gate was in such serious disrepair by 1390 that it had to be demolished. Its successor, the present Stonebow and Guildhall, was not finished for over a century. Some rebuilding of private dwellings took place, but things were getting worse.

There was to be no improvement in the city's economy in the 16th and 17th centuries, and its physical decay became so acute that many houses had to be demolished and rebuilt. The Council, which now met in the Guildhall above the Stonebow, made regular attempts to improve things but achieved only limited success. Among those to whom appeals were made was Cardinal Wolsey; he had been successively Dean and Bishop of Lincoln in 1509-15, and rose to become Lord Chancellor to Henry VIII. The king himself visited in 1541; as is usually the case, the city carried out a general tidy-up and presented gifts to the monarch. He, in turn, agreed to some remission of the civic burdens.

In spite of the damage recently inflicted by those rebelling at Henry's radical proposals to break with the Church of Rome, the King was able to lodge at the Bishop's Palace. The Lincolnshire Rising of 1536 had seen thousands of rebels, also aggrieved by poor harvests and new taxes, gather in Lincoln. The King exhorted them to give up their fight, describing the county as *'one of the most brute and beastly'* shires in the Kingdom. Several of the rebellion's leaders were subsequently executed. The Reformation involved the removal of Cathedral treasures and the dissolution of the city's monastic establishments, which also owned large amounts of land. The City Council was unable to acquire these sites. St. Katherine's Priory, for instance, passed in due course to the Grantham family who built a large mansion in the grounds. The city did, however, manage to take over the Greyfriars water-supply with its conduit and extended it further to a new conduit outside the church of St. Mary-le-Wigford. This structure, still standing, was formed of re-used stone from a chantry in the Carmelite friary.

Action was taken to rationalise the building stock in line with reduced requirements. Only fourteen churches were left after the Union of Parishes in 1549. Many houses were derelict and in a state of collapse. Rebuilding was largely confined to those along the main routes re-using, in part, the redundant fabric from the churches and friaries. Large new houses appeared: several timber-framed buildings of some scale still survive, and brick was introduced, the Chancery in Minster Yard being the best example of its early use in the city. Documents refer constantly to orchards, gardens or *'waste'*. The suburbs contained some farms, and much of the land there returned to fields. The Fossdyke, which had been crucial to the city's success in terms of trade, was in poor condition, but efforts made to improve its state met with only partial success.

The Cathedral remained an important focus of learning and culture. William Byrd, the leading English musician of the Elizabethan era, worked in the Close for a while. The Minster's school itself was merged in 1583 with the local grammar school which choristers attended after their voices broke. Greyfriars became its new base. The Bluecoat School, established by the Christ's Hospital foundation, was initially based from about 1611 in part of St. Mary's Guildhall, before moving in 1623 to a new site on Christ's Hospital Terrace near to the top of Steep Hill.

The 17th Century

The next century was characterized by even more religious and political troubles than in previous periods, but at one level it started positively. King James I was quite taken with the opportunities that the city and its environs provided for sport on a week's visit in 1617. In contrast, his successor Charles I faced some local opposition to his demands for contributions towards the cost of England's involvement in war. In the preamble to a new charter granted in 1628, the city had described itself enthusiastically as *'one of the chiefest seats of our whole Kingdom',* and as a major centre of trading activity.

The events of the Civil War were to inflict more damage on the fabric and in turn on trade. Lincoln's prospects were not helped by its location on the frontier between the opposing sides. The king was well received on his visit to the city in July 1642, but opposition forces were in control soon after his departure. The city changed hands several times. The upper town was pillaged in 1644, but much greater damage was inflicted in 1648 during a second battle. Many of Lincoln's surviving medieval buildings were badly affected. The episcopal

palace was set fire to and became so ruinous that it ceased to be habitable. Two uphill churches were destroyed and others burnt or severely damaged, while the Cathedral itself was subjected to further ravages – especially to its windows, brasses and monuments.

With the Restoration of the monarchy in 1660, the city returned two Royalists as Members of Parliament, but the new king ordered that the town charters should be surrendered in 1684. A replacement was issued in the following year. The Cathedral Chapter had all to be reappointed after the war with the exception of the Archdeacon. One of the newcomers, Dean Honywood, oversaw the fabric repairs and commissioned the new Wren Library. After the Protestant monarchs, William and Mary, succeeded the Catholic James II in 1688, nonconformists were tolerated, and all opened houses; the Quaker Meeting House, built as early as 1689, is still standing. King William's visit to the city in 1695 passed off well, and one outcome was the granting of a new September fair.

Green Shoots?

Increasing demand from the end of the century for the county's wool from the West Riding cloth towns made the Fossdyke's clearance even more urgent. In 1672, the year after a new Act was passed for its re-opening, cargoes were passing through and steadily increasing in scale. There were new mills and maltings. Lincoln was essentially now a one-street town – admittedly a long street which contained some fine houses – but it was beginning to exert an economic influence much wider than that of a market town. It still served as an administrative and social centre for much of the county. The upper city was witnessing the first signs of revival, with repair work on parish churches and major roads. Houses were being modernized. By the end of the century the population was definitely on the increase: a recent estimate suggests a total of about 4500 by 1714.

Revival at Last

The Georgian period witnessed a sustained improvement in Lincoln's economic fortunes that accelerated throughout the 18th century. The Agricultural Revolution was having an effect by 1750, and a further stimulus to the local economy came from improved communications: this was the great era of coach and canal travel. There was an improved life for the wealthy, with a greater variety of goods and social activities including recreations such as horse-racing and balls. Lincoln may have been isolated but the city's ancient remains were visited and described by a growing number of antiquaries. Some ancient monuments had survived in a remarkable state to this period, but much was to be lost from building activity over the next century. Daniel Defoe noted that the best area for trade and business was the steepest part of the hill. Much of the fabric elsewhere in the city remained *'ragged'* (to use Defoe's term) for several decades.

The medieval chapel on High Bridge was removed to widen the road. The construction in 1786 of the 'New Road', later Lindum Road, made the approach to the upper city less demanding. But the reopening of the Fossdyke canal was a greater stimulus. After Richard Ellison had leased the dyke from the council it was back in use in 1744, and Ellison made himself a personal fortune. He was also a partner in Smith's Bank, established in 1775-6, and soon boasting a huge turnover. Lincolnshire's main contribution to the early decades of the Industrial Revolution which was under way in other parts of the country, was – as now – to supply food to these growing populations. The Witham was also improved, and the Brayford developed into a busy port surrounded by warehouses and boat-yards. Much larger vessels, up to fifty tons, could reach the Pool via the Fossdyke by 1820. Although standards for most people were improving, the number of poor also increased, and their living conditions worsened.

Georgian Society and Recreation

For the gentry, on the other hand, this was, on the whole, a good period. Horse-racing transferred to a new course on the Carholme in 1773. The Lincolnshire Handicap was first run here in 1849. Several balls were held each year, one popular venue from 1744 being the new Assembly Rooms on Bailgate. A small theatre existed from 1732, situated near to the Castle. It moved to its present site behind Clasketgate in 1736, and was rebuilt in 1806. Walks and parks were created for fashionable strolls, including Temple Gardens, near the later Usher Gallery, and Besom Park, on the line of the old city wall. The first Lincoln Library began, operating by subscription, and the first permanent newspaper, the *Lincoln, Rutland and Stamford Mercury*, was published in the city in 1784.

Public facilities appeared on a much larger scale. The County Hospital moved near to the top of Steep Hill in 1777 and a new asylum – the Lawn – was established nearby on Union Road in 1820. A new Sessions House at the bottom of Lindum Road was joined by a city prison. A new county prison was built in 1787-91 at the Castle after a report criticising the awfulness of existing conditions. An extension to the rear in the 1840s encompassed the new 'Pentonville' system of solitary confinement. Its unique prison chapel can still be visited. Nearby Shire Hall, built in 1776, suffered subsidence and had to be replaced in 1826 by the present building.

Educational opportunities were still limited, but expanding. National Schools only began to appear early in the 19th century. To the west of the Castle was the House of Industry, where some of the poor were employed; it was replaced by the nearby Union Workhouse in 1837. The Temperance Movement fought strongly against crime and drunkenness, and there were eight Nonconformist chapels by 1826, some of them large enough in due course to accommodate over a thousand worshippers.

By 1801 the city contained over seven thousand inhabitants – for the first time for over five hundred years. The Reform Act of 1832 and the Municipal Corporations Act of 1835 altered the structure of the council, so that it now consisted of twenty-five members, including representatives covering Bail and Close. The new electorate voted in a group of reformers at the next elections.

INDUSTRY AND ACCELERATED GROWTH

The Victorian period ushered in a new era for Lincoln, witnessing the greatest sustained period of growth in the city's history. It followed the arrival of the railways – and the easy availability of coal and iron – that facilitated the development of heavy engineering. Lincoln became home to some large and internationally famous manufacturing companies, initially founded to make agricultural machinery. Rapid growth in work of this nature created social problems but also provided the council – and certain individuals – with the resources to provide public amenities and services. The census of 1911 indicates a population of over 60,000, an urban community that was more socially stratified and regulated than ever before. It required buildings of every type – civic, commercial, ecclesiastical and residential. Some talented architects were involved in their design.

Railways

Lincoln was nearly a railway town of the first rank. The Midland Railway arrived from Nottingham in 1846, and the 'loop' line in 1848 with a route to London via Boston. Although Lincoln was included in eight out of nine possible schemes, the route selected for the main Great Northern Line by-passed the city, instead taking a course closer to the major population centres further west. The construction of the Lincoln to Honington line in 1867 provided another link to London via Grantham, and other east-west routes came via the city. This was the age of the train: the railways' tracks and sidings occupied a huge area, and the rail companies became property owners on a large scale.

Heavy Engineering

The drive to make agriculture more efficient was the critical factor in the creation of Lincoln's principal engineering firms. Four particular companies became major employers, with more than 10,000 workers between them and an international reputation for quality. Clayton and Shuttleworth made steam engines, threshing machines and portable engines which were exported widely to Eastern Europe. Other companies included that of William Foster (later to be associated with the tank) and Robert Robey. Robey's products included winding engines for collieries and electric lighting power for the City of London. Joseph Ruston, a man of considerable commercial flair, travelled widely to market the products of Ruston and Proctor. The firm's mechanical excavators were highly regarded and were employed to dig out the Manchester Ship Canal.

Many of the factories were located close to the river both up- and down-stream of the city centre. There was a range of other industries across the city, some of them necessitated by its expansion: for new building, brick and tile were needed, and limestone, ironstone and sand and gravel were still extracted close to the edge of the city. Steam-driven mills were introduced and factories producing fertilisers were built, both to serve local agriculture. Others supplied social and cultural needs: breweries were widespread, and boats, organs and bicycles were manufactured.

The retail trade, particularly for clothing and foodstuffs, developed commensurately. The Co-operative Stores were first established in 1861 before expanding into many branches, and department stores arrived, along with Boots the Chemists. The Cornmarket was moved to a new building west of Sincil Street in 1846, still the main market area. The Cattle Market was given a new, more convenient, location on Monks Road in 1849. There were also horse and sheep fairs.

Population Growth and Physical Expansion

The speed of growth of the city is clearly discernible on the City Surveyor J. S. Padley's five maps of the city made between

1819 and 1883. The area north of the Arboretum and around to Nettleham Road saw the greatest area of villas for the middle classes. As the city spread further, many of the more affluent members of society went to live in the suburbs. Some of the great industrial magnates had huge residences built in town or in parks on the edge of it. For the manual workers, new housing developments were to be found in the Monks Road area and to either side of lower High Street, locations convenient for the factories. A horse-drawn tram began operation to Bracebridge in 1883, primarily to transport workers; it was replaced in 1906 by an electric version. Developments along Burton Road and in the West End followed at the end of the century. Many of the new units were barely adequate, and poor living conditions were exacerbated by the pollution caused by industry, the general filthy conditions in the town, and an unsanitary water supply.

The new structures of the period were principally of brick, with slate roofs. Some incorporated cast-iron girders. The hospital was moved to its present site between Greetwell Road and the hillside in 1878. A new prison was built nearby, on the north side of Greetwell Road, at about the same time. There were new barracks on Burton Road for the Lincolnshire Regiment in 1878. The growing populations demanded larger churches, and several were rebuilt, one of the first being at St. Nicholas in Newport to a design by George Gilbert Scott. St. Swithin's, whose first phase was finished in 1870, and St. Peter

in Eastgate were others. A new Roman Catholic Church of St. Hugh arose in 1893, and several larger nonconformist chapels were also created: in 1851, more than half of those who worshipped were non-Church of England (Weslyans were particularly numerous), while up to a half of Anglicans did not attend church.

POLITICAL CHANGE

Although the second Reform Bill of 1867 brought the working class into the electorate, many of the elected members of the council still belonged to the traditional middle classes, and were rather detached from the problems of the poor. They were slow to levy a rate and to implement the Public Health Act of 1858. Some services had existed for some years, provided by private companies. Street-lighting by gas reduced the incidence of night-time crime. A cemetery was created towards Canwick in 1856. Responsibility for sewerage was imposed by the Government in 1876. It was only following a devastating typhoid epidemic in 1904-5 that serious action was taken to improve Lincoln's water. Eventually a rate was introduced to provide essential services including gas, water, electricity and the library. Living and working conditions slowly began to improve, partly thanks to the Lincoln Trades and Labour Council, established in 1892.

Education and Recreation

Many new schools opened in the second half of the 19th century, some under the auspices of the Church. They included a School of Art and Science, based on Monks Road. It diversified to offer technical subjects, and was renamed the City School. The Grammar School moved to a new site on Wragby Road in 1907, where it later merged with the Christ's Hospital School for Girls, founded on Lindum Road in 1892 to a design of the talented local architect, William Watkins. There was also a diocesan training college (now Bishop Grosseteste University College), based in Newport. A College of Theology took over the former County Hospital site on Wordsworth Street. Library facilities were also expanded. The first Public Library was created in a room over the Butter Market in 1894; in 1913 it was transferred to the present site in Free School Lane. The leading local newspaper, *The Lincolnshire Echo,* celebrated its centenary in 1993.

By the turn of the century, opportunities for recreation included the races, parks, theatre and music hall, football and cricket matches, and trips by train to the seaside. In 1872, the City Council created the Arboretum, twelve acres of ornamental gardens on the hillside north of Monks Road. The new park had a moralistic purpose: to encourage families to relax together and especially to keep fathers away from the public house and other temptations. Groups came from neighbouring towns to admire the scene.

The Last Century

Lincoln lost nearly a thousand men in the Great War of 1914-18. The city also made a huge contribution to the war effort in machine production. Its factories were chosen to develop and build the first tanks, as well as being prolific producers of aeroplanes, using a workforce that included many women. The firm of William Foster had specialised in agricultural machinery, and had tested tractors with caterpillar tracks, seen as the best means of crossing the intractable ground of Northern France. In 1915 the Government asked Foster's to produce, in secret, an armoured version suitable for those conditions. The prototype was soon being tested. Full-scale production of an improved version began early in 1916, and by September it was in action. Foster's workforce leapt from 350 to about 2000.

A roughly contemporary development during the war years was the involvement of Ruston-Proctor in the production of military aircraft, including testing from an aerodrome on West Common. In all, nearly three thousand were produced. Together with the other local companies, Lincoln made more aeroplane engines during the war than any other city in Britain, and was the third largest manufacturer of aircraft.

After local firms had been fully stretched during the war, with its end they faced a slump. The re-branded Ruston-Hornsby now diversified into producing cars of excellent build quality, but their high price meant that they could not compete with the mass market, and production soon came to an end. Another type of vehicle saved the firm: small diesel locomotives were turned out until mid-century, many used for mining. A link up with an American partner facilitated the development of the legendary Ruston-Bucyrus excavators, using engines made in Lincoln. Even the name Ruston has now been lost; most recently, it has become part of Siemens.

More production was, of course, necessary in 1939-45, and engines, tanks and tractors, as well as munitions were turned out in great number. The RAF established many bases in the county that played important roles in World War II. Many of the airmen and their families based locally provided good business for local traders and attractions. The RAF remains a prominent feature in its life: the bases at Scampton and Waddington a little to north and south of Lincoln, house the Red Arrows display team and the AWACS early warning aircraft respectively.

In the past few decades, however, as elsewhere in Britain, the manufacturing sector has struggled against international competition and much in the way of skills and employment has been lost.

EXPANSION AT THE FRINGES

Population growth continued in the 20th century, but at a slower rate as people justifiably demanded more space. Many city dwellers moved out to surrounding villages. The worst slums in town were cleared and large new estates developed. These included inter-war schemes at St. Giles on the north-eastern fringe and at Boultham to the south-west. Land for the Swanpool Garden Suburb was acquired by Ruston with the philanthropic intention that his workforce would be share-holders. Only part of it was ever built, but it still became a successful neighbourhood and is now a Conservation Area. Other extensive estates have grown up at Birchwood and the Ermine, west and north of the city respectively, and in North Hykeham adjoining its southern edge (still, anomalously, not strictly part of the city).

MODERN ARCHITECTURE

Lincoln can boast some notable Edwardian buildings but much of the city's mid- and later 20th century architecture is uninspiring. There are some exceptions, such as St. John's church on Ermine East. Much of the post-war architecture within the city centre, especially that in the concrete 'brutalistic' style, has not been universally acclaimed, and already some of those structures have been replaced or clad in softer or more appealing materials. More successful recent additions have included the Central Library rebuilding, the St. Mark's development, the new museum (The Collection) and several of the new structures built by the University including its imaginative conversion of former railway structures.

Thanks to the pressure exerted by local historical and architectural associations, several historic buildings were saved and restored in mid-century and fortunately the forces of preservation also prevailed when the Roman Newport Arch was seriously damaged in 1964. Conservation, supported by English Heritage and the Heritage Lottery Fund, is clearly the way forward, but new uses are sometimes difficult to find for historic buildings and, while they remain empty, they are at risk. It is generally accepted that there is much in the historic environment that the community values, apart from the economic arguments. Lincoln has been successful in securing grant aid, and several parties are still working together on more schemes; they will need to do so for many years yet.

SUGGESTED FURTHER READING

There are now several one-volume histories of Lincoln, and countless books on particular aspects. The most substantial account, with a detailed bibliography, takes an archaeological viewpoint: David Stocker (editor), *The City by the Pool* (Oxbow Books, 2003). The substance of this work has been incorporated into a Townscape Assessment, and this has now been made available online at www.heritageconnectlincoln.com.

This title is one in a new series by **Cottage Publications**.
For more information and to see our other titles, please visit our website
www.cottage-publications.com
or alternatively you can contact us as follows:–

Telephone: +44 (0)28 9188 8033
Fax: +44 (0)28 9188 8063

Cottage Publications
is an imprint of
Laurel Cottage Ltd.,
15 Ballyhay Road,
Donaghadee, Co. Down,
N. Ireland, BT21 0NG